Enjoy !

# ADVANCE PRAISE

*"Praise for Dr. D.'s research! By translating years of research and practice into a model anyone can access, Dr. D. provides a rich experience for the reader that involves rediscovering key life moments that influence how a story gets formed and performed in the real world. Story You Mean It reminds us of the importance of prioritizing the art and science of storytelling in our lives and how transformative and value-affirming such storytelling can be."*

—CHIP CONLEY, AUTHOR OF *PEAK*; TWO-TIME *NEW YORK TIMES* BESTSELLING AUTHOR OF *EMOTIONAL EQUATIONS* AND *WISDOM @ WORK*; FOUNDER AND FORMER CEO, JOIE DE VIVRE HOSPITALITY

*"This book takes you through the obstacle course of life and helps you make sense of it, then build and tell your story. It's important because without a method or system, people—as I say—tend to stay on the couch! This book gets you moving forward in life. I focus on getting people off the couch and moving again, and Dr. D. gets people moving too…by guiding them to build and tell a personal story that keeps them on their real true north."*

—JOE DE SENA, FOUNDER AND CEO, SPARTAN, THE WORLD'S LEADING OBSTACLE RACE; TWO-TIME *NEW YORK TIMES* BESTSELLING AUTHOR

*"Dr. D.'s work, Story Like You Mean It, gives people a structure to guide exploring their own key life moments en route to constructing a story worth listening to. Dr. D. played a significant role during our CatalystCreativ Catalyst Weeks as a part of the $350 million revitalization of downtown Las Vegas. His unique method of teaching storytelling not only inspired all of the guests who participated, but he shifted the entire trajectory of our experiences. He changed the lives of so many people by teaching them to think about themselves and the world at large in an empowered way."*

—AMANDA SLAVIN, CO-FOUNDER,
CATALYSTCREATIV; *FORBES* 30 UNDER 30

*"People love to tell stories about their lives, and these storytelling moments give great pleasure to both the teller and the listener. But stories are more than that. Personalized storytelling can be the way forward to living a more effective and fruitful life. Story Like You Mean It offers a methodology for learning from life experiences and highlights a pathway for personal and professional development all in one. Dr. D. has worked to develop this approach for many years, and this work makes his insights readily available to multigenerational and multicultural audiences."*

—DENNIS T. JAFFE, PhD, FAMILY BUSINESS
FELLOW, SMITH FAMILY BUSINESS INITIATIVE AT
CORNELL UNIVERSITY; CLINICAL PSYCHOLOGIST

*"As an advocate for storytelling to help build awareness for needed lung cancer research, I used Dr. D. and the PeakStorytelling model to not only help lead survivor advocates to share their experiences with others to lobby for research and funding but also to help each person feel more positive about*

*their own path of life, embrace who they are, and illustrate their unique value.*"

—CHRIS DRAFT, CEO AND PRESIDENT, CHRIS
DRAFT FAMILY FOUNDATION; NFL ALUMNUS

"*Story Like You Mean It is brilliant. The book showcases a perfect approach to shaping how personalized stories are shared. Dr. D.'s sense of others invites even me, who stories by nature, to consider how powerful language helps us showcase our unique gifts, talents, and motivations. It propels us to consider our past stories and how those previous experiences direct and carve one's future. It is a clear and profoundly purposeful method of storytelling that sculpts value and worth in a world that has limited attention span and time. [This book] is a must-read if you want to get to know yourself better, learn how to get people to listen to what you have to say, and change your life.*"

—DR. WANDA HEADING GRANT, VICE PRESIDENT
OF DIVERSITY, EQUITY, AND INCLUSION, CLINICAL
ASSOCIATE PROFESSOR, COLLEGE OF EDUCATION
AND SOCIAL SERVICE, UNIVERSITY OF VERMONT

"*Our personal story underlies and impacts every decision we make and how we react to the world outside of ourselves. Story Like You Mean It offers a process and the tools to awaken us to our authentic selves and understand the narrative that drives everything from our leadership style to the way we engage in critical decision making and our shared experiences. I highly recommend it.*"

—MARGARET McKENZIE, MD, PRESIDENT,
CLEVELAND CLINIC SOUTH POINTE; ASSOCIATE
PROFESSOR OF SURGERY, CLEVELAND CLINIC LERNER
COLLEGE OF MEDICINE, CLEVELAND, OHIO

STORY LIKE YOU MEAN IT

# STORY
## LIKE YOU
## MEAN IT

HOW TO BUILD AND USE YOUR
**PERSONAL NARRATIVE**
**TO ILLUSTRATE**
WHO YOU REALLY ARE

# DR. DENNIS REBELO

**LIONCREST**
PUBLISHING

STORY LIKE YOU MEAN IT
*How to Build and Use Your Personal Narrative
to Illustrate Who You Really Are*

ISBN    978-1-5445-1964-7  *Hardcover*
         978-1-5445-1962-3  *Paperback*
         978-1-5445-1963-0  *Ebook*
         978-1-5445-1965-4  *Audiobook*

*To my students at all ages and stages of life: without you, my story would be less rich—and impossible.*

# CONTENTS

# CONTENTS

# INTRODUCTION

"Tell me about yourself."

The person is taken by surprise. They hesitate, then start to mutter something about what school they went to, what jobs they've done, what their ambitions are. It sounds like website copy. It's boilerplate; it's an overpracticed, highly memorized elevator pitch. It has no flow, no character, no interest.

Maybe it's not a complete train wreck, but they get the order tangled up and you see the frustration on their face as they realize they've lost the listener's interest. It's awkward for both of them.

They're stumbling their tails off, and they finally blurt out, "How about you?"

The other person is ready. She explains in a few sentences the decisions and actions in her life, showing how she has overcome obstacles and worked with others to have ended up in this exact place at this exact time on her way to her next goal. This time, the listeners get it. They pay attention, they buy into the story, they form a connection with the speaker.

We've all had times when we've been more like the first speaker, right? We can see that the other person isn't really listening. We kick ourselves and think "I should have said this" or "Why didn't I say that?"

It doesn't have to be like that.

## SHAPE THE CONVERSATION

Imagine walking into a room, say for a conference, job interview, or a business development meeting. Maybe you're a leader in your field. Maybe you're just looking to make your name for yourself. Whatever the situation, the stakes are high. You really want to be heard. You're prepped and ready. And then, inevitably—because it is almost inevitable—someone asks about what you've been up to.

"Tell me about yourself."

You're being given the chance to shape how someone judges you. You don't want to miss it. An uninspired story isn't just a poor story; it's a missed opportunity.

I'm going to show you how to take that opportunity to tell your PeakStory—the story that not only shows your value and worth but also shows how you got here and where you're going. And you're going to learn a lot more about yourself, your abilities, and your motivations.

When someone says, "Tell me about yourself," what they're

really saying is, "Show me what you can add to my life. Show me why I should listen to you."

It's the same when they say, "Tell me about your company." That's not what they really mean. What they really mean is, "Tell me about yourself—and why I should listen to you tell me about your company."

We've all been there. Sometimes it happens to you; sometimes you watch it happen to someone else. One way or another, it happens to all of us, sooner or later. We get put on the spot because someone wants to know something that's not about our job, not about our product—but about *us*.

The only reason we keep getting away with the same humdrum responses is that everyone else comes up with the same thing.

Whenever we walk into a conference, an interview, an orientation for work or school, or a sales meeting, people are wondering, "What value do you bring to the conference, the school, the service? Why are you trying to sell this thing or this service?" When they ask you about yourself, you see in their eyes that they want to hear something positive about *you*—but you default to the soundtrack: "I've got a dog and a cat named Felix, and they fight a lot." "I really like the school. Good story: my aunt went here." "I'm really glad to be here working for ABC Fidelity, Elemental LLC, PQR, Z [whatever…plug in the name]. I've been with the company for eight years, really great company to work with. And like, yeah, it's good to be here."

In terms of telling your own story, this is the net sum zero.

Today, everyone talks about what we're netting out in terms of energy. How much energy are we using? How much are we replacing? It's the same with telling our stories. Either you took energy away from the people in the room, or you brought positive energy to the room. Nobody ever walks away saying, "Boy, I met John. I'm completely neutral from having met John."

## STORYPATHING™

Your story is a great source of energy. Any chance to tell it is an opportunity to provide energy to others. But the energy doesn't come from the story alone. It comes from the value your story suggests you bring. That might be commercial value, social value, your value as a friend. It makes other people more willing to listen to you. And that's all that anybody needs, right? In an interview, a sales meeting, or at a conference or seminar.

We want people to listen.

What makes people listen is knowing that the very thing that you're doing right now, you're supposed to be doing. That you're aligned with your story. That this is where your story has brought you.

When you tell your story, it provides not only an anchor in the past but also a compass that points to where you're heading. It brings you to your current reality en route to a "somewhere" you're projecting. Psychologists call this making a *provisional identity claim*. I call it *storypathing*.

Storypathing says to the listener, "Here's where I've been. Here's where I am. Here's where I'm headed."

That stakes your provisional claim right there.

The next bit goes like this: "It all makes sense, doesn't it? You feel energized. And don't you want to support me? You think I have value and worth, and my story has shown that. Thanks. Because it's my story, and I've thought about it and I've activated it."

By storypathing, by making sense of where you've been and where you're headed, you can show that you have more engagement and more value wherever you land because your story aligns with who you are.

If I understand that the very thing you're trying to do right now is what you're supposed to be doing, I will grant you some sort of opportunity. I'll give you space or support. I'll introduce you to more people. People have no problem extending a meeting or doing anything they can to help somebody get to this place of alignment.

We have an impulse to support people who are good at things. We buy tickets to see people who are good at singing; we go to plays to see good actors. If you're good at telling your own story, people will buy in. They'll see not only that you're good at what you're doing but also that you have evidence of your value because the evidence is embedded in the story.

You're talking the talk because you walked the walk.

### "CAN I DO IT?"

You might look at your life and worry that you don't have the kind of experiences that will let you storypath. Wrong!

If you've lived twelve years on the planet or ninety-two, you can tell your story to show your value.

We all can. Storytelling isn't foreign to us. We did it habitually when we were younger. For whatever reason, we fell out of practice, but it's still latent within us. It's an unused muscle we can start using again.

It's not just telling a story, like relating an anecdote or having a chat. It's more than arriving at a meeting and saying the traffic was really bad so I'm a little bit late. That says nothing about you.

Storypathing is an act of self-authorship, but it's also a method for discerning lived experiences. Anyone can drift through a "normal" life. They're not that engaged in the world, and the world's not that interested in them. When you storypath, the world makes more sense because you're making more sense of it. (Trust me, it all makes sense!)

Storypathing helps a person live what some psychologists call a phenomenal life—not meaning phenomenal as in fantastic but phenomenal as in full of phenomena: in other words, facts, occurrences, and circumstances. A branch of psychology called phenomenology teaches basically that a phenomenal life is a life of full awareness of one's feelings and connections and how they occurred.

In other words, everything starts with *you*.

## YOUR PEAKSTORY

Storypathing allows you to put together your best narrative in the best way to create your PeakStory.

PeakStorytelling is a method of storypathing to identify and prioritize life moments to build our story, which we then share with others. It gathers self-event connections, which are moments and experiences that echo through the rest of our lives, and it overcomes two main obstacles that prevent us from telling our PeakStory.

First, most of our lives don't include a lot of purposeful reflection that allows us to drill down into the meaning of what's happened in the past. Although many people achieve moments of reflection through therapy, a spiritual approach, or being out in nature, that reflection isn't systematic. Those moments fall short because they're disconnected. They can't tell your story *over time*.

PeakStorytelling begins with self-reflection. We can't express ourselves unless we can make sense of ourselves. Otherwise, we might as well just post pictures on Instagram that reveal next to nothing about us. You can't judge someone from a picture; you can't show worth through a picture. Yet, we take that course because it's just far easier to post a picture than to reflect deeply on moments in time.

Systematic, purposeful reflection holds the key to PeakStorytelling. We have to go inside before we go out. Me search is the ultimate research.

Second, we've abandoned our desire to be heard because we're surrounded by resistance to telling our stories—everyone's posting photos and we follow suit. We've given up our ability to explain who we are. We resist telling our stories because no one else is doing it. And we don't have a tool to work through resistance in a sensible way. That's why we need to activate the story muscle to start it moving again.

When you learn to storypath, the conscious process of bringing your identity together with your narrative becomes your story over time. Storypathing leverages the PeakStory method to select which parts of your story to tell to get people to listen, understand, and appreciate.

## CREATING A SYSTEM

The PeakStory structure is a purposeful, research-driven methodology that gets you to the stuff that matters in your own story. It grew out of my PhD dissertation, which brought together two disciplines: humanistic psychology and organizational systems. Combining those two fields gave me not only an understanding of the structure of the brain but also an awareness of how to assemble pieces of one's life in sensible ways for high-stakes moments.

To put it simply, there are occasions when it really matters that you're heard for who you are and why you add value. When you need to be a story wizard.

As humans, we're all handlers and collectors of lived experiences. Well, those experiences are the raw material of your story.

Over and over while I was researching, I watched people get a chance to tell their story and goof it up. Or maybe miss it altogether.

Unless they were the leader, of course, because the leader always gets to tell his or her story and is never challenged, because who's going to stop someone when we all need their signature on a paycheck, right? One reason I came up with the PeakStory method is because, my whole life, I've seen storytelling privileges given to people who are in power, yet not to those people who want to be honored as experts or value creators.

That's not good for anyone or for any business.

One of my aims is to take research-based data and turn it into something that works in the real world or to take what I observe in the real world and turn it into a system. A system is repeatable. That makes it useful and gives it value.

A woman I coached recently, Whitney, put it like this: "If something you see in life is beautiful, it's worth duplicating. It needs a system that can help that duplication become possible."

Well, that describes what I do. And that system for duplication became my obsession (and eventually the PeakStory method). I became hypervigilant about people's stories, and I began to see patterns.

## THREE TYPES OF STORY

I realized that when people used strong stories about self-preservation or overcoming obstacles, those stories woke listeners up so they could see value. I called those hero stories.

People still couldn't see full value, however, because we don't just want somebody to be a hero warrior. We also want to feel that somebody can work with others.

So I started to identify these working-together stories, which I named collaborative stories.

When people put together hero and collaborative stories, I saw they were not only explaining how they had come to be where they were but also getting insights into how they could live a better version of their inner selves.

I call the stories that combine hero and collaborative the super-self or virtuous story. These are good-work stories, good-life stories.

I realized that if you can tell all three types of story, then your listener can understand:

- You're credible (Hero)
- You can work with others (Collaborative)
- You're en route to the most virtuous version of yourself (Virtuous)

You've also made yourself more relational by backtracking your story and knowing those multiple self-event connections. Because those self-event connections are rooted in the real world and real experiences.

As I started to notice these real experiences, I started to nuance how to onboard them into a story that would become a PeakStory. I learned to nuance storytelling performance.

When you tell a provocative, relationally impactful story, you get people's attention and they want to talk to you more. Period. You get them to see value in you for who you are, and it's liberating. I felt changed. I saw how others changed.

I wrote my dissertation, but those stories kept coming into play whenever I was coaching people in public speaking. So I took my ideas and created a couple of visuals and started pressing them into classes around public speaking. People became liberated by them. I watched students hit resistance to storypathing, then learn to go to their formative experiences, unpack them, and be relationally changed by them. People started saying, "I thought this was going to be a public-speaking class, but it transformed my life."

So I came up with the PeakStory method.

It's based on academic research, backed by over a decade of teaching around public speaking and coaching leaders of organizations in high-stakes moments. I co-founded the Sports Mind Institute. Some NFL people called me in. Companies called me in, such as Sennheiser, the German audio company. Academics. Police. Students. I've led educational activities here, there, and wherever. I've spoken outside of Zappos as part of their downtown community program. I have online students on US Navy ships and on the other side of the world.

Now it's your turn. Are you excited? You should be. You've gotten to know a little about who I am, and now I'm going to help you get to know yourself a whole lot better—and how to introduce your new self to others.

Ready? Let's start this adventure together.

## EXERCISE: YOUR STORY JOURNAL

The PeakStory method is just that—a method. It's a practical way to achieve something.

And practical means practice.

So if you think this is a regular book that you're going to read in your easy chair or on the couch, you're wrong. This is not that kind of book. This book is going to show you stuff, tell you stuff, explain stuff. You'll need to grab a pen or your laptop.

That way, you get the full deal. When I coach people or they do the method online, they get interaction. That's why you'll find exercises between each chapter in this book. You need to think about stuff, write about it, put it into action.

You're not being shortchanged. This is it. This is the method. But to get the most out of this book, be prepared to put some work in.

It's nothing to be worried about. It won't feel like work. It's fun because it's all me search.

Finding out about yourself. What could be easier?

The exercises bring together theory, which is the thinking, with practice, which is the doing.

You might feel they slow you down. You might feel frustrated because you want to get right to telling your PeakStory.

My advice is this. Don't rush. One step leads to the next step. Trust me. This works.

The first exercise couldn't be easier. It's not even an exercise.

You'll need a journal to keep track of your progress. It could be anything. You could take a trip to the stationer's for a fancy notebook, or root through your desk to find an old legal pad, or grab a handful of sheets of paper you can clip together. You could just create a new file on your computer or tablet.

You just need somewhere to make notes, do the exercises, and refer back to them.

Once you've got that, we're ready to start storypathing.

---

# CHAPTER 1

——

# THE CASE FOR STORYTELLING

*From the Garden of Eden*
*to the branches of Macintosh*
*apple picking has always come at a great cost*
*iPod iMac iPhone iChat*
*I can do all of these things without making eye contact*
—MARSHALL DAVIS JONES, FROM
HIS POEM "TOUCHSCREEN"

When was the last time you *really* connected with someone's story?

It probably wasn't recently.

That's no surprise. There's not enough storytelling today. We have few invitations to tell our story, and when they turn up, we're often like, "Er, um, okay, let me see…" because we're out of practice.

It's nobody's fault. It's the way things are. But it's not healthy. We're losing the ability to make meaningful relationships with others. And the worst thing is, you keep wearing the same pattern down over and over again: the chance to speak comes, and you miss it. The version of yourself you put forward isn't the best you. In systems thinking, this sort of repetition is called a virtuous snowball effect, if it's good, or a vicious snowball effect, if the results are negative.

Failing to tell your story well is a vicious snowball effect because you just keep repeating the cycle. And the more you repeat it, the more your brain feels comfortable in terms of neuroplasticity, which is its physical ability to reshape how you think. Your brain doesn't seem to want to change at times. It prefers familiarity and comfort. Who wouldn't want to feel comfortable in a situation where people don't know you and the stakes are high? You don't want to try something new.

So you're going to repeat the same story that didn't interest listeners last time or the time before, because it's comfortable. But the reality is that the comfort creates no reward for you or the listener, does it?

Because you're not creating relationships.

## MOVE AWAY FROM ROUTINE

Sherry Turkle, a professor at MIT who studies technology, connectedness, and the human condition, describes the modern world like this: "We expect more from technology and less from each other."

The way I put it is that our world is overconnected but underrelational.

Technology connects us to everyone in every place. It lets

me teach people on the other side of the United States or in Europe. I appreciate it, of course, but I think everyone sometimes despairs of how it gets in the way of our ability to think or relate deeply.

Our devices connect us wherever we want to be mentally wherever we are physically. This tricks us into thinking that we're involved, but that's just not the case. Technology has not advanced enough, in the words of my friend Marshall Davis Jones, to make us human again. It pulls us away from reflection and from each other. Our thoughts, frankly, are not as deep as they once were or could be.

We're losing the ability to forge relationships at the very time it's easier than ever for us to make more connections.

Technology pulls us away from reflection about those moments in our lives that have some sort of weight or significance in informing who we are—our self-events or self-event connections. Without these connections, we become a thin version of ourselves rather than a fully matured version, which means we present ourselves like a "beyond perfect" Instagram picture that doesn't actually capture the context and depth of who we really are.

It's a partial image. It's like falling in love with a new house online, then going to the neighborhood and seeing there's an oil refinery across the street or they're mining rocks. Or maybe you're a bit meh, but you go take a look and the house has a wonderful view over a lake, or a fine park next door, or is close to the train station. In some cases, a fuller picture reveals problems, but in others, it adds value.

## OBSTACLES TO STORY

To form relationships, you need to add value, but the people you want to listen are busy. They're distracted by their own technology-driven lives. Technology doesn't only decrease our self-reflection. It also reduces the amount of time we have to tell our story. It quashes our empathy, or our ability to relate to those whose stories we hear, and that's something else we need to recover.

Technology and the lack of opportunities for meaningful reflection are not the only barriers to meaningful storytelling. It's also habitual. According to the science writer Charles Duhigg, there's a social cue for most forms of interaction. The cue triggers a routine, and then we get a reward.

In public speaking, the social cue is somebody saying, "Okay, now it's your turn." Or maybe it's just a look, or the person before you has finished speaking, and now it's your turn. But those chances don't come along too often, and when they do, they're usually fairly routine.

Most nonroutine opportunities are reserved for the leaders, right? You know, the people in charge of the "talking stick." Not for those who want to show their own value.

The social cues tend to reward those who adhere to the routine. People who say more or less just what everybody else said, and what everyone has said before. You're rewarded with more opportunity to speak out if you stick to the script, if you keep things comfortable.

But do you want comfort? Or do you want to be known as

being valuable? Do you want a technological connection or a deep relationship based on your worth and value?

It's hard to abandon comfort, so you're going to resist to telling your story. The good news is that the PeakStory method removes the resistance for you. It has for people from fourteen years old up to ninety years old, so you can feel just fine about it.

Relax, you'll be good. No anxiety required.

## TAKE YOUR SWING

When the moment comes, when people's eyes rise above their devices, you have to be ready to step in the batter's box and swing.

"Why are you standing in front of me?" "Tell me about yourself." One strike and you're out. They're looking down again.

Think about the next moment when you'll likely need to tell your story. Is it a client development conversation? Are you entering a new job? Are you returning as an alum? Are you a guest speaker at a conference or on Zoom? Are you in a high-stakes networking environment?

You need a story and you don't quite have it. You can't think of anything different to say, so you say what everyone else says. You're going to play the same music everyone else is playing. You're going to tell the story formatted like everybody else. And you're going to get a response like everybody else. Unless you're ready to show your value in a PeakStory.

## GENERATIVE DIALOGUE

With a PeakStory, you're going to awaken the listener and start to increase the likelihood of generative dialogue. That's a to-and-from between the speaker and listener that gets you somewhere new. It breaks new ground.

When you do that, you're going to start to win people over through personal story. And they'll start unveiling their life moments as well. Whether it's in their spoken language, body language, or tone of voice, you'll notice signs that suggest they understand you. They *get* you.

The very essence of storytelling is creating this loop between the teller and the listener. Even if you're speaking to a large audience, a dialogical quality can come out. While you're talking, you should be feeling more personally connected and relationally significant to others. You'll see this yourself soon enough by way of watching others respond to you. And that should make you feel liberated.

Think of it this way. Every time you repeat the expected story, every time you're singing the same old song, it's as if your finger is digging a groove into the sand on the beach, deeper and deeper. So when it's time to talk, which is when the water comes up, it rolls right into that pathway. Right? The same old path.

The wrong path.

You need to draw a new path. You need to reroute your patterns of referencing key elements of who you are in your story, whether it's a sixty-second, ninety-second, three-and-a-half-minute, or eight-minute telling, or it's prolonged across a thirty-minute speech.

## WHY STORY?

I've seen many examples of the transformative nature of telling your own story. They surprise even me, right, and it's *my* method.

Take a student of mine named Hannah, who was an immigrant to this country. She was a female wrestler who wrestled against the boys, so you can tell she was very confident. At the beginning of the class, when I first introduced the system, she took a pause. "Whoa, wait a minute. I've got to really rethink. I can't just be confident in speaking. I actually have to speak *to* something."

So she went a little deeper and looked at her life. Lo and behold, about nine weeks later, at the end of the class, she said to me almost nonchalantly, "Hey, Doc. I told my story in that interview with the Rhode Island Foundation and I got the scholarship." I said, "Wait, you did what?" She said, "Yeah, I told my story, just like we did in class."

And I said, "Wait a minute. Whoa. Hannah told her story and got a scholarship. Was it a good scholarship?" She goes, "Oh yeah, it's $20,000." And I said, "Twenty thousand dollars to tell your story?" And she said, "Well, yeah, $20,000 a year at any school I want." I said, "Wait a minute. It's four years, so that's $80,000! Congratulations."

She said, "Yeah, it really feels good to be myself and be rewarded for it. Now I want to talk to you about telling my story for the internship I want."

I told her, "Ooh, you're addicted to story!"

This is the sort of thing that can happen with the PeakStory method. It can help overcome problems. It has proven outcomes.

## YOU WRITE THE STORY

Turning into a PeakStoryteller comes at a little bit of a cost, but it's only really your time. You're worth it. In return, it sparks meaning, remembrance, and nostalgia. It also allows you to become a screenwriter in your own Netflix or Amazon Prime series, so you start to build up your life episodes like those TV sizzlers to get people's interest. You can turn the episodes up or down. You get to be the director, the producer, the editor, all using your lived moments.

You start to realize that there's meaning in your life events and that you can shape that meaning. You feel better about yourself, with more personal connection. Your body language changes when you meet people, introduce yourself, do client development meetings, give a speech as a leader, a CEO, a business owner. Your body no longer lies or undermines you. Your voice tone improves. You're calm, less twitchy. You're not blinking or flailing your hands. You tell your own story, and that makes you feel more settled.

When you resist telling your PeakStory, you continue down the same groove, just like everyone else. You know that you're not like everyone else, but the more you repeat the same old story, the deeper the groove. Your lived experiences lie lost beneath dirt and leaves and brush, leaving you emotionally unsettled because you're not saying who you truly are.

## STORY FOR BUSINESS

When people hear your PeakStory, they start to hear the humanistic side of your narrative. But they also hear the business applications.

Our lived experiences are connected to those of other people, so your story sparks a response that's not purely analytical. It's beyond "What's your balance sheet?" or "What's your return on investment?" Straightaway, there's a human connection, so this becomes a more humanistic business exchange.

Isn't that what we all want from our high-stakes face-to-face conversations, whether they're live or online? Don't we want our work to be grounded in our nature as humans?

We may want that outcome, but there's still a challenge: "How do I form or synthesize my story?"

When I started creating the PeakStory model, I asked Howard Gardner, the Hobbs Professor of Cognition and Education at Harvard, about the use of storytelling in business. Gardner is well known for his theory of multiple intelligences. He followed up that work with his idea of the "five minds for the future." Gardner notes that everyone will have to develop these "five minds," which he summarizes as a *disciplined mind*, to learn at least one profession; a *synthesizing mind*, to organize massive amounts of information; a *creating mind*, to investigate new phenomena and unasked questions; a *respect-ful mind*, to appreciate differences between human beings; and an *ethical mind*, to fulfill our obligations as citizens.

Gardner clearly saw the value of what would become the PeakStory model to enable entrepreneurs to communicate their particular synthesis of knowledge to sell their ideas. He believed the approach I offered was needed, writing, "I agree that synthesis is vital for the business entrepreneur and you rightly point out that the entrepreneur needs to be able to communicate their synthesis to others. Borrowing a term from education, the entrepreneur needs pedagogical knowledge about how to synthesize to those with varying degrees of knowledge or expertise."

The PeakStory method provides just what Gardner suggests is needed: a map, system, and process for helping business folks with the challenge of synthesizing their value.

## ADDING VALUE

In business, speaking poorly means you don't get another shot. No one invites you back if it takes seventeen reps to get your story straight. No one says, "That didn't go so well, but you can try to sell to me again." No one says, "It was a poor interview, but no problem, make another appointment. I'll be glad to send you a link to my calendar and you can book five more hours for your practice on me since I have nothing else to do other than listen to you."

You need to show up ready to honor not just your own story but also the human being with whom you're about to speak. Let's not blow their time. Let's give them a real show. Tell them your sizzlers: past, near past, now, likely future. That's really it. The sizzlers tell the story.

At this point, you start to rediscover that storytelling muscle. You start to become hyperconscious of moments where you can speak to your future and explain your path.

Once you start spotting the pieces, which you inevitably will, you can start putting them together, though it's going to take you a little while. You're going to get really enlivened to *go live* fast, but there's still work to do. There's no place to hide once you go live—take the time to prepare first.

For now, look out for those moments that add value to your life, such as overcoming an obstacle or working creatively with others. The more you see, the more of them you'll notice. It's like when you buy a pair of shoes in a particular style and you start to realize how many other people have those same shoes. Or you buy a Volkswagen and you start to realize how many people drive a Volkswagen Golf.

Identifying these other examples gives validation to our choice. It's a cycle. Your heightened awareness leads to focus and that leads to reward: in this case, validation. That's what will happen with the PeakStory method. You become more focused, you present your story, and you get a reward.

## KEEPING IT REAL

TV is full of stories.

Why can we watch previews on Netflix or other streaming services? So we can tell whether a show is worth watching, right? So we can evaluate the story.

What's interesting is how quickly we do it. Think about it. You watch a minute or two of a sizzler, and you decide that you're in or out. That's how we make purchase decisions, buying in or not.

Why did you buy this book? Maybe it was the title. Maybe it

was my bio in the back: "Dr. D. has worked with people in pro sports." Something struck you and you bought the book. You signed up to reading about fifty thousand words based on reading, what, one hundred words? Two hundred?

By the way, how much work do you think went into the title and the biography? A lot. Because they're the only chance to make you think the book might be worth your time.

A Netflix sizzler is the same—and so is storytelling. When you tell someone your story, you're really asking them to see that you have value. That you deserve their time or money, or both. That they should show you to somebody who could hire you, use your services, somebody in their company who could engage in a consulting conversation, some advisor. You're lobbying for value because value earns opportunity.

## THE PRICE OF VALUE

All sorts of modern studies show that people want to be valued at work. Today's workers want meaningful work and self-expression.

Where can they get it? I mean the way to expressing themselves meaningfully about work? We don't give it to them in the HR department. We don't give it to them in college. One school that wanted the PeakStory program didn't even have a communication or rhetoric department.

Imagine the advantage you'll have once you can speak your PeakStory. Those who can't speak follow the masses, the same old groove. But if you can speak, you can activate agency and free will. You can start to author your own life and be more actively involved in it.

## SELF-DETERMINATION THEORY

In psychology, this self-authoring aligns perfectly with what's called self-determination theory. It's really the ability to go and get something out of life.

Self-determination theory has three parts: autonomy, relatedness, and competence.

Current research building on seminal work in self-determination theory found that humans want to be psychologically well and feel good in terms of our motivation, development, and wellness. At a basic level, we need to feel like we can make our own choices, which is autonomy. Then we need to be able to have relationships with others. And we also need to become competent in something.

As we'll see in the next chapter, the PeakStorytelling method will get you to a place where you're acknowledging these three parts—autonomy, relatedness, and competence— you're being acknowledged in turn by your narrative.

---

## EXERCISE: BE MORE ALIEN

This is our first real exercise. Remember, it's not a chore. It involves a little effort, but that's because I'm going to ask you to think differently than usual about things. It might take a bit of getting used to!

I want to make you more aware of story: how many times you get to tell your own, and how many times you hear somebody else tell theirs.

To do this, you're going to become an ethnologist, which is the academic term for someone who studies people. We don't need to bother with the qualifications; just imagine you're an alien who has just landed on Earth and is trying to figure out all about humans by watching—and *listening*.

First, choose a location where you can eavesdrop. Maybe you're at a conference. You might be killing time in the park or at an airport. Maybe you're sitting with a coffee in a café. You might be in your office.

It's harder in places that use social distancing, but ideally it needs to be somewhere where you can hear people introduce themselves or bring their friends up to speed. Failing a real-life situation, try listening to chat shows or interviews on the TV or radio.

Listen to what people say. Think about where the stories are located. Are they at the beginning of phone calls? Are they part of formal introductions or a voice teleconference call with multiple parties, a video-based call, a live interaction?

What types of stories or moments within stories are standing out? What makes you zone out?

You're looking for hits and misses, strikes and balls. Do you notice someone completely failing to hit the target?

If you want to kick it up a notch, what do you see in the body language of the listener? Or the speaker? Are you seeing signs that someone is zoning out?

Think about what you hear and see. What are you learning about this alien species? Which stories make connections and which fail to do so?

Make a list of both and write it in your journal. Take notes of anything that stood out.

You're tuning your social radar—and your social radar is also your *story* radar.

---

# CHAPTER 2

# UNDERSTAND YOUR STORY, UNDERSTAND YOURSELF

*"It is an ironic habit of human beings to run faster when we have lost our way."*

—Rollo May

In the past, storytelling always came with power.

When you think about the people who got to tell their stories, it was always teachers and principals, the leaders of departments or organizations, politicians or celebrities. Throughout our lives, it's been the people in charge who have had the storytelling privileges. They're the same people who control the meeting: what time it starts, what time it ends, whether it happens late.

(Which is fine by us. As long as they still sign the paycheck, right?)

That's not the deal anymore. A Willis Towers and Watson study of employee experience in 2014 found that workers today want a qualitatively different outcome than workers of past generations. They're not just looking for salary or promotion. They're searching for meaningful work.

Welcome to the world of the flip.

We no longer see work as a situation with leaders versus followers; instead, everyone is a member with a voice. Student voices matter in universities, colleges, and schools. Worker voices matter in organizations. Those who lacked privileges have become the equals of those who had the power—and often become more powerful.

## STORY MATTERS

Now that everyone has a voice and a story, it doesn't make your story less important. It makes it more important. If every voice matters, every story matters.

As the hierarchy of the top-down organization disappears, everyone gets more opportunity to tell their story. In the world of the flip, everyone's a leader.

Listen to this observation from a key leadership professor, Warren Bennis, who passed away a few years ago: "Becoming a leader is synonymous with becoming yourself; it is precisely that simple and it is also that difficult."

Well, we're going to make it easier.

Let me tell you why I love that quote. Because a leader is anyone who can influence others, so becoming a leader is also synonymous with learning how to influence people. There's only one way to do that: communication. Which means that you can also become yourself by learning to communicate in a way that influences others (combined, to be sure, with putting in some work).

That's what storytelling does. It helps us become ourselves. It allows us to answer the age-old question, "Who am I anyway?"

And, in doing so, "Tell me about yourself."

The PeakStorytelling method teaches us how to reclaim our voice to tell our story. It shows us how our experiences of identity shape the way we present ourselves to the world—and the way the world accepts us.

Identity can be meaningfully brought into being through rhetoric, by which I don't mean fancy elocution and elucidation. Rhetoric is simply a name for approaching the spoken word through a method—PeakStorytelling—that provides an apparatus for telling your story.

## IT'S ALL ABOUT YOU

We've known for decades that telling your story is a way to better understand yourself. Psychologists such as Abraham Maslow and Rollo May have been writing for decades about how self-expression can release people from their cages.

It's an approach broadly termed humanism. At its heart is the notion that understanding yourself encourages positive selfishness: using self-knowledge to best achieve your goals, always with an awareness of others and your relationships, of course. Positive selfishness encourages us to ask ourselves,

"How am I going to know myself better en route to claiming the thing I want: the job, the interview, the school, the promotion, the responsibility?"

I'm not going to jump into the research as much as I could. That's too much detail.

To put it simply, "Hey, you matter."

You always mattered. I know that. But in the world of the flip, it's more acceptable. Society says that it's okay for you to matter.

Take the rise of social media. Now that everyone has a platform, everyone is busy trying to tell his or her own story through the ideal picture or the ideal post. They're looking for something that says, "I am kind of this person here in this… Instagram picture, this Facebook post, this tweet, this TED Talk video…whatever is the platform of the day."

People use social media to project a version of themselves. We've already seen that psychologists call this a provisional identity claim. It's intended to give an impression of you to anyone who sees the picture or post—but it's provisional because it can be changed when they find out more about you or meet you. A provisional identity claim doesn't tell your full story. In effect, it just says, "I think this is kind of cool."

Look at your friends' Instagram posts. Do they ever say anything more meaningful than that? It's as if someone is asked, "Tell me about yourself" and says, "Hey, I went surfing on Tuesday and it was awesome. The sun was just over the horizon, man. It was first light."

That's not storytelling. It's a report. It doesn't reveal all of you.

## SELF-EVENT CONNECTIONS

The PeakStory method is based on self-event connections.

If you don't know the phrase, no cause for alarm. Self-events are meaningful moments in your life that link to wider influences on you. Self-event connections, in other words, are the evidence that something matters or mattered to you. They come from all areas of our life: our work, our family and friends, our recreation, our spiritual lives. To express yourself in your PeakStory, you need to study yourself, discover these self-event connections, and unpack what they mean.

We've all learned to keep these threads separate in our lives. We don't cross lanes. Mommy and Daddy probably taught you not to. (And they signed your paycheck, right? Their house, their rules.) Your PeakStory teaches you that those lanes aren't impenetrable. Leaders cross them all the time to create the best version of themselves.

Well, now it's not just the CEO who can cross lanes. Now that storytelling is more democratized, we all can.

## CLAIMING POWER

If becoming a leader is synonymous with becoming oneself, becoming oneself must also be synonymous with becoming a leader. Which is another way of saying that you gain power. There are different sorts of power. Position power comes from title or position, say, within an organization. Coercive power means you have the ability to punish people for not doing something, and reward power means you can reward them if they do.

We can't all access those forms of power, but there's one power we *can* access: expert power. Anyone can put expertise into their story—but some ways are more effective than others. And once you can do it effectively, you can achieve referent power, too: the kind of power that comes from being likable and being able to foster good relationships. As a leader and communicator, you wind up with the two best sources of power. Who wants to be known as the person with the title who has the power to give out the carrots and the sticks? That's not how people want to be led today.

If you simply say, "I have a degree," that's a bit flat, like "I have a PhD and MBA. I went to this school, I have this certification." Instead of saying, "Here's my degree from ABC tech school," how much better to say that you were handed down how to be a designer-craftsman from your grandfather, who was a master woodworker-cabinetmaker. That story underlines your claim to expertise and does so with a likable style. It illustrates how to access the types of power people seek in those they trust.

You get that. It's straightforward. Maybe you can already see how you can twist part of your own story to make a bit more of a claim. You want to go out and try it.

Don't.

You're not ready to rush in and say, "Hey, this is why my identity has value." We have to do the work, people.

Before we can embed self-event connections into storytelling, we have to find out which ones are important. We have to dive backward and ask, "Who am I?"

## THE MAGNIFICENT NINE

Self-event connections aren't always easy to identify because we're all running pretty fast in our lives. You've had hundreds or thousands of these foundational experiences. The Peak-Story method will help you find just a handful.

How many? Nine, that's all. If you can identify nine experiences, you're in the game. You're playing to win: to win attention, to win the listener's ear. To win value points because you showed that you have value and worth.

Once you've identified these experiences, I'll show you how to examine, expand, and label them to identify their ingredients. What competency did you show you were good at? What were your motivations? What was the "power of the place" you were in? What kind of people were around you?

Breathe easy. It's not some kind of academic assignment.

It's just looking back at your own life in a slightly different way.

## YOUR OWN HIGHLIGHT REEL

Most of the time, we're so busy that we communicate without much reflection: "Hey, I went surfing on Tuesday and it was awesome." But there are lived experiences just underneath the surface, so we need to unearth them so we can embed them in our story. They're the sizzlers that make you think, "Ooh, I want to see that movie." We need to pick out the bits that gain interest, that get us noticed. That makes the dog do the doggy head tilt.

The story doesn't have to be radically unexpected, although it might be, but it sparks attention to get the audience out of their anesthetic state. It tells them that you understand your story and therefore you understand yourself. That understanding is embodied in the different moments they didn't expect to show up. They expected references to your degree, where you live, the number of kids—the standard drone. Instead, they got the real stuff. It slaps them in the head, tells them to wake up.

Doggy head tilt.

Human beings have a wonderful social radar. Even if it's been on snooze for a while, we wake up when somebody diverts from the standard story.

Just check out why some videos become viral. It's because they're earnest, they're clear, and they get attention.

## EXPLORING LIVED LIFE

When we've identified your experiences, we're going to tag them for how useful they can be for telling your story. We'll rank them. This one's a nine. This one's maybe a five; let me stick with it for a while and think. This one's just a two. I can't include it, but it did help me understand something about myself.

The way to do that is to go back to the experience, think about it, then think about it again. Think and rethink.

To use the vocabulary of phenomenology, a phenomenon is anything significant that has happened in your life. Edmund Husserl, who founded the approach in the early 1900s, believed that if a person examined and reexamined their lives, they would have a heightened awareness of their experiences. I originally called the PeakStory method *phenomenological storytelling* because it honors that approach. I learned to use phenomenology in grad school as a social science research method to study the quality of lived experiences.

From an academic standpoint, it was really cool. From a practical standpoint, it was even cooler. It just made sense.

Maybe you're saying to yourself, "Well, I've thought about these bits of my life before." Sure you have. It's your life, after all.

But have you rethought it three or four or five times? Have you journaled about it? Have you identified the ingredients of the lived experience? Have you thought about the people and places involved, the mental muscles, the motivation? Did you use leadership, creativity, adaptability, your analytical skillset? Did competencies pair together to make you an inspirational leader? Did you do it reactively to some trigger, or did you do it proactively?

Those are the kinds of questions you'll learn to ask as you start to explore your makeup. You'll learn to see what value to give to past experiences, what universal competencies they express, and how they create positive energy.

## IDENTITY CONTENT

The key to your story is identity content. How does an experience add to the creation of your identity?

A psychology researcher named Jane Dutton and her colleagues looked at this question in 2010. They suggested that people have the best chance to proclaim a positive identity by aligning with one of six different behaviors. A person can validate their positive identity claim by identifying with one of just six positive types: virtuous, favorable, progressive, adaptive, balanced, and complimentary—all of which, by the way, can also be elements of a PeakStory.

It seemed simple, but it led me to ask myself, "How does someone structure storytelling to include such lived experiences?"

I realized that the real story here is that people want identity content. They want to understand other people and their worth, and they want the identity content to be supported by evidence.

Look at it like this. A good lawyer cites precedents as evidence from old cases when they're lobbying the judge to believe them. Maybe you're not an inspirational orator, as seen in trials on TV, but you can humbly insert your lived experiences when storytelling—and those experiences also have value in making your case.

That's why we'll learn how to think about your intention so that you can pick the right evidence from your life for your particular audience and, in turn, get what you want from them in response.

In this method, there's a big tilt to me search. Me search is the best research (I like to add that because it's true).

Even by simply using PeakStorytelling methodology to build your story, you're more self-aware. When you decide to tell your story, you'll get more. You're relationally more in tune. You're contextually more intelligent because you understand the context of your storytelling at a particular time, place, to a specific person or group of people while preserving your intention.

## ELIMINATE THE NEGATIVE

Let's talk about what can go wrong.

Think about how everybody else tells their story. The language they use. "I'm very credentialized in this field." "I've had my CFA for a number of years." "I've worked for Lehman Brothers." "Edward Jones was a friend of my grandfather."

You know what? When you put it like that, I don't care. Right? I don't care. No one does.

In psychology, this kind of elevator pitch awakens in the mind of a listener what's called a negative cognitive script. It's like an undesirable reaction that lights up in someone's brain. Subconsciously, it encourages people to judge you and your behaviors in a negative way.

Another way to put it is, "Hell, you put me to sleep. I zoned out there."

People in similar work-identity positions sometimes use the same language sets—and that repetition creates a negative cognitive script. It's like anesthesia for the listener. Worse, it can cause the listener to take cover or run and hide. Mentally, they shut the speaker down and out.

So the question is, have you done the me search/research to tell a story people will hear, or are you going to let others have the power to judge you?

I'll give you an example of the power of negative cognitive scripts so that you'll be sure that you got it. Say you're looking for a car, maybe a Camry or a BMW or whatever it might be. Online, you've seen dozens, hundreds, even thousands of these cars. But when you show up to a dealership and somebody approaches you and asks, "Can I help you?" the first thing you do is respond by saying, "No, I'm just looking."

Nonsense! Of course they can help you. That's why you're there.

But instead, you've lied to this person who might be, say, a retired schoolteacher, a former cop, a straight-A student. Why? Because you've heard language that we perceive as negative—"Can I help you?"—within the context of a car dealership, which has always been riddled with negative associations.

I feel bad for car people. So many of them are such good people, and they get negated because the negative script is so strong. You actually don't even want to know about why they might be selling cars. You don't care. You won't listen.

That's how a work role can create a massive, prejudicial mis-characterization of who someone is.

## THE THIN SLICE

The writer Malcolm Gladwell talks about the concept of the

thin slice. I call it a misslice. It describes looking at some-body and instead of seeing the whole thing, you just see a slice—and it's the wrong slice. So instead of judging a person correctly, you get it wrong, based on the wrong evidence.

That's what happens if you don't have your story ready. Somebody gives you the liberty of a self-introduction or a high-stakes networking moment, and you flub your story.

Instead, your physical traits, characteristics, and role identity start to overwhelm your story. They squelch anything that you say. They leave the listener with a misslice.

And if all you're going to say is what everybody else says, that serves to validate the negative or nonpositive evaluation.

You could have gotten it right, but you goofed it.

## MEET THE BLUE DOTS

You have to do the work. It starts with studying your self-event connections and formative experiences.

My term is blue dots. When I did the original PeakStory dia-gram on a whiteboard, I grabbed a blue marker to color the dots representing these moments. I stuck to it. Blue makes me feel better. It makes me think of a blue-sky moment when you see clearly. Life is good. So people in my classes started to call them blue dots.

That's what we call them.

You could have a hundred blue-dot moments, but our work

has discovered that it's good to focus on about nine. From those nine, you're going to pick three. As you go on, you may rotate through the other dots, so they matter, too, but you'll use three in the work you'll do here.

### Joining the Dots

It may be that you don't recognize your blue dots at the moment. That's no cause for worry because we're going to help you. Just be aware that three will emerge. And *you'll* pick them. We can't predict them.

What those three are depends on when and where you tell your story.

Telling your story is situational. It's targeted. Like a custom video-streaming moment, it shows a particular character at a particular time. So if I'm speaking to somebody who's in the US Navy versus a nonengineer who loves the arts and who does development work in the Berkshires around MASS MoCA, my story would not accent my time at LaSalle Military Academy in the same way. I could choose another formative experience completely.

You don't have to use the same blue dots in every story you tell. At the same time, don't worry if you do. Guess what? You'll have consistency, and your story can stand some repetition.

Think about it. If you hear someone's story over and over again, you don't say, "Oh, I've heard that story before." Instead, if somebody uses credentials such as their positions or qualifications over and over again, they become embedded. So, in fact, repeating lived experiences makes you feel more connected to your own narrative.

## KNOW WHERE YOU'RE GOING

Take a look at the diagram.

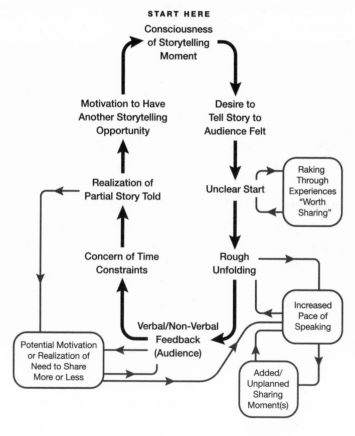

I presented this diagram at an international conference at Oxford University to illustrate the flow of someone attempting to "tell their story." Pay attention to the "raking through" section and the relationship between the act of "raking through" and being "unclear" at the beginning and how that impacts the unfolding of the person's attempt to answer the question, "Tell me about yourself."

It basically shows why people have trouble introducing themselves. I ask students why that is. "You knew that you were going to come here. You knew this class was a leadership development program."

Then I show them this. And the key part of this is the little circle that says, "Raking through experiences 'worth sharing.'" If you've already vetted your experiences in relation to where you are now, you don't have to worry when you tell your story. You can almost autopilot (later, we'll get into how to tell your story in a way that gives you space to tune it while you're saying it).

You don't have to struggle and have an unclear start and a rough unfolding. You don't want to be that person because that person simply stands where they started.

You can just let the story unfold as people react. And then you go to the next dot and then the next dot because you already know your story is ascending. It's going from hero to collaborative to virtuous.

Those three dots are your PeakStory.

They say, "My value is perfectly aligned with what you, my listener or listeners, are looking for right now. I have value and worth at this moment in time, and you see it clearly. It's clear to me and to you. Look at me. It all makes sense, right? You want to continue the conversation or learn more about me? Hire me? Accept me into your school, program, or institute? You can see that I'm the person you want."

That's your PeakStory.

## EXERCISE: BACK TO THE FUTURE

Storypathing means looking at events or moments in terms of how they might contribute to our overall story. Don't worry. You already do it automatically. We all do. We just don't put it into words.

You also self-narrate. Self-narration is a language performance that's anchored in truth and creates a value statement. You want to tell your story in such a way that people walk away from you and say, "Wow, that's great. There's someone who really has value."

Again, you already know how to do this. That's why you notice when people give positive reactions to things you post on social media. That's why a like feels good.

What about seeing your own value?

Try going back to your memory feeds, when Facebook or Instagram prompts you and says this was a year ago or this was five years ago. If you're old school, look at an old photo album.

You're trying to start understanding how your brain at a particular moment in the past considered something that might be important to your story.

Try to find one or two photos that really just stand out or strike you from a particular period.

Why did you pick these two? How do these two pictures capture your identity?

Write an analysis of each image in your story journal. Time to unpack more from each picture.

Ask yourself:

- What is it about the pictures that captures your identity? Was it where you were? Was it what you were doing, what you were working on, whom you were with?
- Was it an inflection point in your career, your college experience, your high school days?
- Was it just freewheeling fun at a time when you were usually focused on outcomes? Was it a moment where you could let go? Or was it that you were exploring or creating something new?
- Were you acting as a team, or were you alone?
- Were you taking a risk on yourself, or were you supporting somebody?

Analyzing the images in this way is the first step toward thinking about the moments that will make up your story and how you're going to present them to your listeners.

---

# CHAPTER 3

———

# PRESENTING YOUR STORY

*"Communication leads to community, that is, to understanding, intimacy, and mutual valuing."*

—ROLLO MAY

Presenting your personal story is not as simple a task as it might seem. It needs to bring together your personal identity with your work story, which is a challenge, but the good news is that it will be worth the effort in the end. Once we're past this stage, you'll be able to start building your story.

Figuring out what your story is is only part of the process. The other part is telling it effectively. This takes work. Like a good screenwriter putting together an episode, you have to reflect and plan, consider your audience, and bring the pieces together.

Telling your story might look very different to some people than others. No worries. The PeakStory method works for everyone. We'll help you find the key parts of your story and build them out so you can use them whatever your reasoning for storytelling may be.

## IDENTITY WRANGLING

The good news is that if you are able to launch into *story* versus starting with *let me tell you a story* when someone asks, "Who are you anyway?" the chances are very good that you're going to hook them.

I call it identity wrangling because identity has always been seen in different ways. At one end of the continuum, people see identity as fixed; at the other end, they see identity as a construct that is constantly unfolding. Although it's true that everyone has a certain neurology—a certain temperament and certain baseline competencies or ways of thinking—it's also true that life unfolds and changes things.

Our social identity, or self-identity, is certainly the result of the interaction between the two, between how we're born and how we change. Sometimes people say, "Well, this is just who I am."

It's probably not.

But the great thing is that now it's you holding the pen, using the keyboard, or shouting through the megaphone. You're directing your own story. You get to control how much of the story you let out.

So you might say, I was born in a particular way, in a particular place with particular tendencies and motivations. Maybe I needed attention and didn't get it as a kid. And so I started performing and I became more of an author-entertainer, where I use communication and creativity and leadership. I still need attention today. I still need to be good at something, but I can shift how I do that because I have agency and autonomy.

Looking from your past to the now or near now and then the future, you can start to come up with possibilities for how you'll live, work, and be in that next chapter of your life. Some options you'll see straightaway. Or you may have to put some effort into adding some visualization to your future. You may find many variations are needed to get you to get a sense of this future of yours, rather than a single fixed "next" something. One approach that can be helpful is to iterate many possible options: living in a particular neighborhood or place; recreating differently by hiking or being by the beach; raising horses; or teaching or mentoring for a nonprofit. Write a list of all the possibilities. Bullet them out.

In phenomenology, we call these options *imagined variations.*

Why? Because you'll have to—in some cases—imagine or develop those possible next moments in your life (that's self-authorship for ya!) that you find both plausible and worthwhile. Good news! At this point, you'll have some understanding of what drives you internally, the competencies, people, and places where you'd like to do your work and live your life.

Of course, this is not a social science experiment. This is your life. But the phrase "imagined variations" is helpful because it helps us see what might be. So you have to imagine variations based on the now, near now, near past, and the way past that are likely to continue your plotline so that your story is relevant, prevalent, and sense making.

## A CASE STUDY

One of my clients was doing premed at medical school but

decided to switch to an MBA program instead. Today, he's an executive at a pharma company.

When we started sorting his story, he said, "I realized I don't know how I even include that my dad was a doctor. It sounds sort of like I'm kissing other doctors' butts when I say that."

He didn't tell the doctors he met that his father was a doctor because he didn't know what to do with the information. He didn't know how to make it relevant, prevalent, and sense making. How did it make sense within his own story? He'd moved from premed to pharma, but he didn't realize the reasons.

He knew there was some sort of connection between what he did and his family's background in medicine, but he didn't have the tools to process what it might be.

So we worked on the story together and went back over his plotline.

This time, he said, "Okay, now I see that I like the challenge of achieving and producing, which means I like getting things done. As a doctor, that takes a long time. So I like that I can influence medicine through an MBA perspective. Through business, I can still work with people who are like my dad but also have a quicker impact as a leader-producer. And if I could help drugs get to market more quickly, then I was naturally inclined to do that. So my motivation is to connect leadership and organization to my work.

"I know how things work, and I can get things done every day. At the same time, I'm honoring research with clinical trials and bringing new drugs to market, because that's where my organization and leadership skills can come into play."

Now that he had made the link in his story, people were like, wow, this guy honors medicine; he grew up in a medical household. And so he could interview and get the job that he wanted in pharma, which was in a startup that made rapid change, rather than the job that would merely pay the bills.

## THE WRONG SIDE OF THE LAW

Part of the PeakStory method is to show you how to take parts of your life that don't seem to make sense now and see how they fit into a story that is relevant, prevalent, and sense making.

Take another example. I once had a student who had been in prison. He was a college graduate who had a few cocktails and decided he was going to move a police car. That's not a good idea if you're a black male in a white town in New England.

Really not a good idea.

So this guy wanted to get a job mentoring and helping others, in particular in a college setting.

How was he going to make sense of that in his story?

When we worked through the method, it revealed that he was an explorer but an overactive one. He had no guardrails. So the process helped him say, "Look, my exploration got me into trouble because I didn't understand the rumble strip. That's the warning track that alerts you to the edge of the highway so you don't drift off. It says, 'You're about to go off the road,' but I didn't understand. So that's exactly what I did."

So this guy came to understand that, and he told his story and he was able to progress. Now he speaks nationally as an advocate for incarcerated folks who are denied certification possibilities, whether it's in physical therapy or healthcare or whatever. He also teaches elements of storypathing in a class called Pivot the Hustle inside the Rhode Island Department of Corrections in coordination with Roger Williams University.

He got that gig in education that he wanted; he's now in front of the class doing the mentoring he wanted to do for others.

By the way, that's the class I used to teach when I met him.

So storypathing both helped him ready himself for public speaking and also allowed him to take stock of his internal narrative and those off-kilter moments where his competencies were knocking him out of balance.

When the thing that pushes you forward also throws you into a ditch, you need to learn how to tune that competency. That's just what he did.

PeakStorytelling has been particularly effective for people who are incarcerated. My colleague James Monteiro, who has received funding from a nonprofit supported by the singer John Legend, started the Reentry Campus Program. It helps individuals who are incarcerated reenter society with educational programs to help them into college and career pathways. James uses the PeakStory method to help individuals understand their own narrative and their formative experiences—hero, collaborative, and virtuous—so they can have their own PeakStory as opposed to being tempted to borrow someone else's story for motivation. The PeakStory model helps people come up with their own powerful story, and they get to possess it for life. They can take stock of their own capacity to gain success and engagement in the world.

## THE DIFFERENCE MAKER

Whether it's an executive in pharma or someone in prison, a schoolkid learning English as a second language or a student at Roger Williams, everyone who has gone through the program has found a way to articulate their identity in the real world by way of story.

Even though this is an inside job, it has external consequences.

The great thing is that finding a way to tell your story is not random. It's the opposite. It's codifiable. That means we can teach other people how to do it. We can teach *you* how to do it.

And it's a difference maker.

It's a difference maker sometimes in getting funding for your nonprofit, getting the promotion you want, getting into the school you want. In the world of stand-up comedy, it's the difference between getting the front row laughing and getting the entire house laughing. It's an engagement thing. It shows you reached everyone.

## INSTANT FEEDBACK

When you tell your PeakStory, you'll start to understand the feedback loop. Your listener is going to give you immediate feedback.

That's unusual. You're used to not getting feedback because you usually go in and tell a dry story that wakes up negative cognitive scripts. It sounds more or less like everybody else in your workforce or business sector. That means you never get feedback, because no one is going to tell you, "Boy, that's a bit uninteresting. You sound like everybody else."

By individualizing your story, you'll create a signature that is unique. It's your narrative imprint. So you release your story with ease, grace, and honor fueled by the confidence that comes from knowing those authentically identified moments. And those real-life moments come alive as you transfer them from your head to the paper and from doing the work on paper into the ears of others.

## GROUNDED IN TRUTH

There are elements of some formative experiences that maybe don't show us in our best light. Not for public consumption, right?

Don't lie about them. Your PeakStory value is grounded in truth. That's why others can't question it and you can have confidence in it. Instead of lying, we can flatten the story. We don't accentuate areas that are not in alignment to the audience or the telling. If you go too heavy in one area, ask yourself whether that content is disruptive to your positive value claim. If you identify a moment that has all the right juice but also has something that's not so great, maybe don't unpack all of its qualities.

Take my client who moved the police car. Perhaps he might say, "I had a short time out years ago where I kind of went out of balance and I was pushing limits. In fact, I moved someone's car. I didn't want to steal it; I just wanted to mess with them and see how far I could go. Let's just say, it got me into a little bit of trouble because they hadn't really consented." He doesn't have to say that he moved a police car if he's at some national summit in Washington, DC, but he might if he's speaking to incarcerated people. They're different situations.

So we learn when to blow up a blue dot or expand it during our telling, and when to flatten it.


## FITTING TOGETHER

Now that you're thinking about blue dots, maybe you're thinking, "Hey, I have this part of my story that I think I want to tell, but I don't know how it even fits."

In my case, that would be figuring out how my BMX bike riding as a kid fits with the fact that I'm now a professor. So my task is to see how that self-event connection is relevant today. Once I understand that myself, when I tell others how it fits, they will accept it.

In this case, my blue dot has to do with creativity, pushing limits, and actually doing the work, jumping the bikes. So then I taught other people how to make the jumps. Now I can see that's why I was a teacher from the time I was a kid. When I tell other people the story, they shrug their shoulders and turn their palms up and say, "Right, he's always been a teacher. He even taught other kids how to ride a bike."

You go back to something that was clearly important, a blue dot, and you join it up to lead toward now or to the near future, to your peak.

Depending on where you are in your life when you investigate your own lived experiences, you're going to see different things. Because my perspective is based on the lived experience, I'm going to understand all the nuances, but I might carry it forward with a different utility.

To go back to elements of my story, let's revisit my bike riding. I'm not telling it *now* as it was *then*. Did I say I did it to compete? No. That didn't enter it. I didn't need that detail because that's not what the experience is to me now. At the time, it was about winning trophies. Now it's about me being a teacher, me being one of the first to do something. The young professor, the young experimenter.

## FAILURE TO LEARN

It took decades of teaching people in companies for me to realize that there are some people who don't actually want to learn. They just want to work their hours, get their paycheck, and get the heck out.

It's no surprise. Companies and organizations are created as places where we divide people by function. They do that function, and they maybe become a bit automated in their work. They might want to do more, but they're not even invited to meetings because the meetings aren't designated for them.

That's just crazy if people want to contribute. As we've seen in the last chapter, up-and-coming generations are motivated by making a contribution more than they are by the paycheck—but companies haven't caught on to this yet.

There is some good learning happening in companies, but for the most part, there's not.

We're still governed by organizing by division and fracture. That's been the model since the fifties and sixties. It's the model today. Perhaps what we learned about remote learning and motivation theory during the COVID pandemic will help change that. We'll see.

But everybody wants self-expression and to make connections. They want relatedness, autonomy, and competence.

And they want to be known as making a meaningful contribution at work. Research tells us employees most often can create an opportunity for meaningful work during the first hundred days in a new position. That's it. After that, their role in the company is set. It's still possible to change, but it takes a whole lot more effort to change how you're seen, to alter your role in the company after those first hundred days.

## TAKE YOUR TURN

Many people end up in environments where they're never asked to tell their story or get a chance to ascribe value to themselves. There are no cues telling them, "Now it's your turn."

You don't have to sit back and wait for a formal invitation.

Everyone is wondering about who are you anyway. People you work with. People you meet with. The invitation is always there: "Tell me about yourself." So if people give you the right to tell your story a little bit, why aren't you doing it? Don't tap out; tap in.

I know you're capable of interpreting your own lived experiences. You don't need to be a phenomenologist, a psychologist, a social scientist, a PhD, or whatever. Heck, you don't even need me, once I've shown you what to do.

I know that because I've seen this work. I've seen people identify moments and grapple with them and ask the key questions. They say, "Ah, this is why that thing keeps sticking out to me, but I never really knew."

But now they know.

That's what we're going to discover in the next chapter. I've told you about the importance of story and some of the great results people have got from the PeakStory method. Now it's time to examine the method step by step.

If we were in a race car, this is where we would put on our five-point harness. We're going to go off-road sometimes, but you're going to be safe. We've got the right vehicle, which is the PeakStory method. You've got your notebook ready. This is where we get into the big-time stuff.

Let's go.

## EXERCISE: UNPACKING A SYMBOL

In this exercise, I want you to think about your story through symbolic interactionism.

It's an academic phrase for something we all do naturally. We assign meaning to objects that are linked to particular events or times in our lives, like souvenirs from the trip we took or the softball we kept from second grade. We give the objects meaning that is intimately linked to ourselves.

Let's practice.

Look around wherever you're sitting as you read this book. You may be in your den, or in a waiting room, or on public transportation.

Pick the one thing you can see that you would choose if you had to interact with it more than other things. I know it's inanimate. Don't worry, I'm not asking you to make a voice for it or anything. Scan the room for the one thing that could represent who you are and force yourself into that interaction.

It might come naturally. You might need a little coaxing along. Hang in there. Don't give up.

Pick one thing. Is it a fan? Is it a microphone, a watch, a lamp, a picture of a guy holding a fish, some exercise equipment, some Post-it Notes?

A banner or a diploma? A printer in the office? Is it an audio speaker? Is it a glass? Is it a coffee mug? A backpack? A bow tie? A key chain? An old car magazine?

Great. You found it. See how easy that was. Now we're going to up the ante.

Now let your mind travel anywhere outside of where you are physically. Close your eyes and pick one thing that represents who you are, linked to an important part of your life, say between zero and thirteen years of age. (Presumably not from when you were zero.) Choose something that would really tell anyone reading this book about who you are.

In the past, people have chosen footballs, track shoes, a chess or checkers board, a deck of cards. For me, it was my bike because it allowed me freedom. I could get out of my house. I could feel like I was a little bit of an explorer. I could compete and show how I had skills to people who were bigger than me.

You might have several things, but just take one. Go easy on yourself.

Unpack the symbol. Ask yourself why you picked it. What is it? What does it make you think of? What does it represent? Can you think back to a moment in time when it had more relevance, more life connections? When did you first start considering this object in your life? When did you start seeing it? If you took a mental flight back to the past of this object, what would you be looking at? How is that relevant today?

Bang. You've done it. It's that easy because symbols can help you to access moments because we live in a physical world. Stuff, objects, and symbols appeared before words, and they likely help you access meaningful experiences and self-expression from the past.

Write about the symbol in your journal. People sometimes draw the symbol out or describe it, then keep the question and the answers.

We're usually distanced from things that matter. Once we slow down, we can see how they link to events that contributed to our sense of self-identity. There might be something in the moment that's really valuable to your PeakStory.

So great job opening up your brain. Thanks for playing!

# CHAPTER 4

---

# THE PEAK MODEL

*"Experience itself is not science."*

—EDMUND HUSSERL

When we're put on the spot and asked to tell our story, we often hesitate. There's a stutter step, a stumble that you feel in your brain as it tries to search or rake through the garden of life experiences. You're trying to grab one you think is relevant to the audience in front of you, but there is just simply too much pressure because you know your own life so well—of course, because it's *your* life—but you haven't bracketed off the time to identify the moments that are most relevant. It's a sort of meltdown your brain goes into when you feel put on the spot. You're trying to get across a whole life in compressed time.

The PeakStory method can remove this meltdown. It prepares you for your chance for meaningful, purposeful storytelling that captures who you are right now or who you're en route to becoming.

## WHAT STORIES TO TELL?

The first thing to recognize is that there is a hierarchy to different types of experiences that have a different amount of weight in your life. When you can identify, explore, and connect them, they create a powerful story that, when transformed into a performance—remember, by the way, your PeakStory is something you actually tell in the real world—almost paints a magical picture of who you are. And it feels as animated to you the teller as it will to the listener.

There are so many stories; how can we possibly figure out the hierarchy?

Well, the good news is that there's a model that has been around since the 1940s.

## MASLOW'S HIERARCHY

If you've ever taken psychology classes, you've heard of Maslow. And those of you who haven't, Abraham Maslow's life work about human motivation is reduced to one claim to fame that everybody remembers: Maslow's hierarchy of needs.

Maslow argued that human beings are motivated to act and feel like humans. He ranked five stages in which humans need to fulfill their needs to achieve contentment, from basics such as food and shelter at the base of a triangle tapering up to advanced stages such as self-actualization.

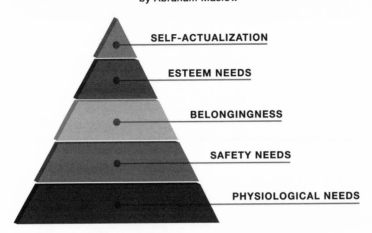

**HIERARCHY OF NEEDS**
by Abraham Maslow

SELF-ACTUALIZATION

ESTEEM NEEDS

BELONGINGNESS

SAFETY NEEDS

PHYSIOLOGICAL NEEDS

Imagine you were to drop in the middle of a territory, like on one of those reality survival shows. Your first thought wouldn't be of making new friends. You would look for food and water. So those basic physiological needs are at the base of Maslow's triangle: food and water. Then comes personal security on various levels: shelter, sleep, and safety. You need protection from the elements. You need rest. You need to be safe.

Maslow's third level was belonging. Remember some point at school where you thought you didn't belong. Or when you entered the workforce, transitioned to a new career, or landed on a college campus; any situation where you felt like you were alone and it didn't feel good because you weren't yet part of the group.

According to Maslow, you don't start to worry about externalized social needs, such as belonging, until you've satisfied your physical needs. After belonging come self-esteem and self-respect, which are internalized needs. At the peak of the triangle, level five, is intellectual satisfaction, which is more about showing our full potential, often through morality, spirituality, and creativity.

## STORY HIERARCHY

People tend to interpret Maslow in many ways, but there are essentially three levels: physiological and safety needs, social needs, and self-actualization.

I based the PeakStory hierarchy on that foundational work. The model is also triangular, built on three layers of story we've already met: hero, collaborative, and virtuous.

As an investigator of your own life, you're going to learn how you—not we, not me, not Dr. D. but *you*—can pick experiences of your life from each layer that have relevance to a particular storytelling moment. In the exercise at the end of the chapter, you'll pick your moments, which you'll remember I call *blue dots*.

## PEAKSTORY MAP

Look at the PeakStory map. In addition to the three layers, the map also has lanes that represent the different roles we take on in our lives:

- Work and education roles, e.g., student, boss, team leader
- Family and friends roles, e.g., parent, carer, partner
- Recreation and hobby roles, e.g., athlete, collector, artist
- Spiritual and nature roles, e.g., meditator, thinker, worshipper

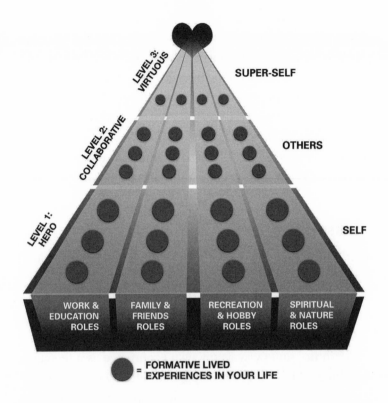

LEVEL 3:
VIRTUOUS

LEVEL 2:
COLLABORATIVE

LEVEL 1:
HERO

SUPER-SELF

OTHERS

SELF

| WORK & EDUCATION ROLES | FAMILY & FRIENDS ROLES | RECREATION & HOBBY ROLES | SPIRITUAL & NATURE ROLES |

● = FORMATIVE LIVED
EXPERIENCES IN YOUR LIFE

The purpose of the story map is to help you identify and sort your blue dots—the moments in your life that you refer to when you tell your story. You'll identify your blue dots in the exercise at the end of this chapter, so stick with me. First, let me explain how they come together to create your PeakStory.

As you identify your blue dots, you'll distribute them in the appropriate layer and lane on the map. Your life is made up of all these different things, so let the blue dots follow. Don't worry about how many; just identify formative experiences. Whatever lane the dot ends up in—work or home or recreation or spiritual—don't sweat it. You'll still be able to refer to those dots and combine them in ways to share a compelling, relevant story at the right moment.

Integration is key to the whole process. Sometimes, who you are as a father is really informative to new hires if you're one of the executives welcoming them to your company. And what you did on a camping trip might be informative if you're a student at a school in the city because it might have relevance in terms of how you think about collaboration. So even though the method has different lanes, don't think of your storytelling as having to have a particular application.

## CLASSIFYING STORIES

Early in my career, I was both a practicing business and career advisor and an academic researcher, and those activities overlapped. I advised students and clients ranging from teenagers through older adults, and I saw connections between their various lived experiences across the roles they held, in the same way as my own experience as a teenager teaching BMX riding skills connected to my experience as an adult professor. In my research, I explored how to understand and provide context to those lived experiences and began to think of them as stories in three categories: hero, collaborative, and virtuous.

## HERO STORIES

In my practical work, I was helping people tell stories about overcoming obstacles; the protagonists of those stories were all heroes. It seemed to me that these hero stories were the basic story we all want to hear and we all want to be able to tell, because everyone experiences them at one point or another, and they represent the human capacity to overcome and survive some condition. They represent strength, grit, and perseverance. They give a person cred.

A hero story attests to your life on the planet as an individual, responsible first and foremost for preserving yourself. You're being a hero to overcome the obstacle in front of you, not necessarily trying to save another human being. The mythology expert Joseph Campbell pointed out that the great stories of literature commonly follow a hero's journey, but you don't have to be a character in a story or a movie to be a hero. Hero stories can be about:

- a physical injury that caused you pain
- developing a technical skill
- having to go overseas and learn Japanese as an English speaker
- getting over a divorce
- having the courage to tell the truth when no one else did
- adapting to a new environment
- completing some physical feat
- standing up to a bully
- letting go instead of clinging on

When a person feels something threatens the fundamental elements of their existence, they become heroic so they can survive. As a hero, their story occupies the lowest level in the PeakStory model, equivalent to the lowest level of Maslow's hierarchy.

## COLLABORATIVE STORIES

If we're never heroic, we will probably be less likely to be invited to a collaborative experience. Without evidence of your grit, perseverance, and courage, others won't want to work with you. Yet, some people move straight to telling a collaborative story, without telling a hero story first. That's like jumping to Maslow's third level without moving through the first and second.

If you go straight into your collaborative story, it has no foundation. "Oh yeah, I understand finance. We worked well together." It's just words. There's no evidence of cred. You have to start with the hero story.

If you've first described how you studied finance in college or learned to balance the cash receipts at your parents' store every night after closing, then I start to think of you differently: "That guy has grit and perseverance. He can work in different environments. His collaboration is valid. He brings value."

In my research, I saw that collaborative stories were the next level of the hierarchy, mirroring Maslow's level of belonging. Collaboration differs from belonging, however. You might think, "Oh, I belong to a company; we create this great product or service." You have a sense of belonging, but that's not yet collaboration. Collaboration is marked by communication, organization, and openness, which show others what you think and compel them to listen.

When you don't know how things work, lack organization, or step on people around you and try to control them, that's not collaborating. It's just being pushy.

The belonging and collaborative phase, in the middle of the PeakStory map, depends on active engagement with other human beings to create something. It could be a school project. It could be a business plan or a marketing plan. It could be a strategic evolution for a particular nonprofit. It could be a plan to find the best caretaking outcome for your elderly parents. That's quite different from "Well, the eldest sibling just bore the brunt."

Collaborative experiences make us more conscious of those people we want to work with—and even those we don't want to work with probably teach us something about collaboration. Working with others in the past informs the people we want to work with and the projects we want to take on in the future. And we identify the skills that need improvement.

## VIRTUOUS STORIES

Our blue dots involving collaboration help us move to the top of the PeakStory map. When the hero moment connects to a collaborative moment or possible future moment in retrospect, we tend to revisit a likely sweet spot and think, *"I love some of this work, this thing I'm doing, this encounter that I'm experiencing. It feels like a peak moment. If I could only do this over and over and over again, I would feel more like myself."* Most times, this sensation is fleeting, like the aroma of coffee in the morning. It's a glimpse of our best selves, the place we want to be—even if we can't get there right now.

The other side is that it might make it clear what you don't want to do, which releases you for the things you do want to do.

The dots on your PeakStory map show the obstacles you overcame at the base level when you became the hero of your story. Overcoming those obstacles led to fruitful or even challenging collaborations and a level of belonging in relationship to other human beings. That prepared you to reach forward into the future for your virtuous moment at the peak.

Like Maslow's triangle, it's a hierarchy: Self. Others. Super-self.

## MOVING UPWARD

The PeakStory method helps us identify moments that move us up the diagram, building toward our self-actualization, the most moral and realized version of ourselves that should be in existence. We personalize our communications to tell the true story of our lives and feel more like ourselves at work. For listeners, our journey along the PeakStory to this work provides the evidentiary basis that validates the work itself, that we have value, and that we have some sort of expertise because of the path we've followed.

Your PeakStory explains how deliberately, and with free agency and self-authorship, you chose this particular moment in time to be in this world and this field of work or studies that you're in right now. Or that you're going to be in in an imagined variation of your story.

You PeakStory is a narrative that takes place over time. The hero moment is past, usually before the age of thirteen. The collaborative moment, depending on your age, is a near or distant past or active present. The virtuous moment lies in the near future in an imagined outcome of the story. It's your about-to chapter or next season of life or work, so to speak.

## THE FOUR LANES

Look again at the PeakStory map. The four lanes help sort our bazillion experiences into four fundamental roles: work and education, family and friends, recreation and hobbies, and nature or spirituality. You have a whole range of experiences.

The four lanes just make them more digestible. They help you find or move toward the virtuous moment in life where you will spend more time doing activities you love.

Because if you're not living a life you love, what a waste, right?

Moving toward your virtuous moment doesn't mean quitting your job, but you might discover that a small shift within the particular space you're in creates a transformative shift in the way in which you feel, do work, and live. And that change influences the way you tell your story.

The lanes remind us that this is about personal as well as professional development. And it's about the development of your speech. The method has many applications in different fields, such as sales, leadership development, and career transition, to name a few. It allows you to see your experiences across the lanes so you aren't weighed down by any particular one.

Let's start by thinking about a moment where you overcame something. Maybe you—like me—had to speak about your science fair project. I grew up in a Catholic Irish family with a Portuguese father; the judgment and punishment I received was often greater than the measure of my childhood mistakes, or at least it felt that way. I carried the fear of making a wrong move into the world at large. When the science fair came around, describing my physics-based science project in an exciting way was a heroic act. I see now that my science fair project in itself wasn't my heroic moment; figuring out how to crack the code to communicate to adults and speak in public without stuttering or feeling judged was.

In fact, I won first place in the state and represented the

state in a US Department of Energy program at Brookhaven National Laboratory that summer. Then I won again the next year and spent a lot of the summer in West Virginia as part of the National Youth Science Camp program. Science became a way forward for me but not really as a career path. It was more important as a way to communicate across audiences. Either way, my heroic moment led to many collaborative moments.

## A MODEL FOR SELF-AUTHORSHIP

In both my research and advisory work, I discovered the PeakStory map was a digestible method to explain how to share a hero moment in a particular storytelling situation, then segue to a collaborative moment, leading to the peak moment. Sometimes the amount of language around each blue dot would change, but combining dots from the layers of hero, collaborative, and virtuous built a PeakStory time after time.

Let's face it, when somebody tells you what they're up to or answers the question, "Tell me about yourself?" they'd better be aligned with whatever they're doing. Otherwise, they're blowing your time because they can't illustrate that they're aligned with the choices to do their work in the first place.

If you're doing what you want to be doing en route to doing something else phenomenal, you can broadcast that with a degree of certainty. You show that you've reflected on your life, and that self-awareness shows me that you're emotionally intelligent, that you're making decisions based on reflective consideration of your own lived experiences. And so I start to think about you, without realizing, as somebody who is self-navigating.

That's the essence of self-authorship, no matter what happened to you in the hero moment. Maybe there was no right answer and what happened might not have been so positive. But the positive outcome was that you saw you had the capability to self-lead and communicate or analyze a scenario. Or be creative, or whatever it was.

In my own life, when I had to introduce myself, I began telling a hero and a collaborative moment en route to what I'm doing right now or about to do. I could see that people were more engaged. And I felt more personally connected to who I was and am becoming.

That's when I knew the model was real. It had academic roots, but it also grew out of practical coaching work around storytelling, leadership development, and speech giving. Everything comes together. I suspected the theoretical model made sense, and when I applied it in practice, it worked.

You, too, are capable of mapping your life this way. You can tell your story through the three phases, with blue dots in each. And every one of these blue-dot moments is made of similar elements, which are motivation, competencies, people, and place. So let's take a closer look at the blue dots and what they mean.

## EXERCISE: COLLECT YOUR DOTS

It's time to start coming up with your stories. Your self-event connections. Your blue dots. Whatever you want to call them.

Look again at the PeakStory map.

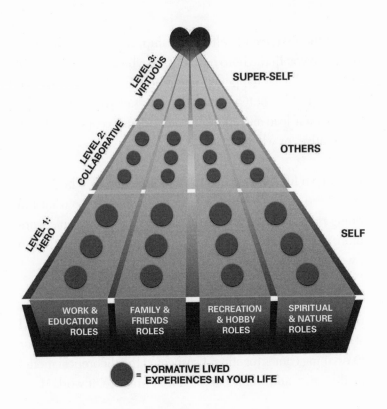

**LEVEL 3: VIRTUOUS**

**SUPER-SELF**

**LEVEL 2: COLLABORATIVE**

**OTHERS**

**LEVEL 1: HERO**

**SELF**

| WORK & EDUCATION ROLES | FAMILY & FRIENDS ROLES | RECREATION & HOBBY ROLES | SPIRITUAL & NATURE ROLES |

= **FORMATIVE LIVED EXPERIENCES IN YOUR LIFE**

You have the three levels: hero, collaborative, virtuous. You have the four lanes: work and education roles, family and friends roles, recreation and hobby roles, spiritual and nature roles.

Remember the different types of story.

*Hero stories*: you've overcome an obstacle that has gained some footing in life, the base of your triangle.

*Collaborative stories*: you've worked with others to create something, an outcome, a plan, a solution.

*Virtuous stories*: You caught sight of what you were doing and you said, "Oh my God, I love this." It could be in the past or the near past, but it's probably an imagined version of the future. It might be a mini moment rather than a full-blown version of the way you want it, or you have an imagined variation of a moment that you're now starting to see.

Now that you're familiar with the types, it's time to come up with some hero, collaborative, and virtuous stories. Ultimately, I want you to identify three of each type of story, and they can come from any lane of the diagram.

If you want to go to four or five, fine. If you want a gold star, you can list seven. But you need to list only three to five and—as with much in life, less is more—better just to list three.

If you need to loosen up your brain, make as long a list as possible, but then start cutting it back. Leave it if you need to, then come back and cut more. The stories don't all have to be positive. You'll be able to find something positive that comes from it, but you don't have to look for the most positive moments. As you reduce your list to three, it will help if you check your stories. Did you drift away from the actual type of story? Was it really heroic? Was it really collaborative? Or really virtuous?

Eventually, you'll be left with the three most important in each type.

I always tell people, check your types. Make sure you're right. That's just me. I'm a double checker. You can then see that hero lights the fuse to understanding collaborative, that spirals up to virtuous. You're starting to lay the bricks in the pathway. You're starting to see connections, maybe from work, maybe from family.

So you're down to your nine blue dots. Write them out on a fresh page of your journal. When we build your PeakStory, I'll have you try them on.

You're going to love it.

---

# CHAPTER 5

## THE STORY STAMP

*"I must achieve internal consistency."*

—Edmund Husserl

You've identified your blue-dot events, the formative experiences that will form the basis of your PeakStory. You're happy with them. At the moment, however, they might not seem to mean much. How do they even relate to one another?

It's time to blow things up. Seriously. We're going to explode each blue-dot event to discover the underlying components. These moments are not singularities. They contain different elements that we can explore in more detail. The best way to do this is by using a systemic, methodical approach to examining our own lives.

### THE STORY STAMP

Refer to the Story Stamp diagram here. It's the tool I've come up with to analyze blue-dot events, and I've found it the best way to understand how useful they are for telling your story.

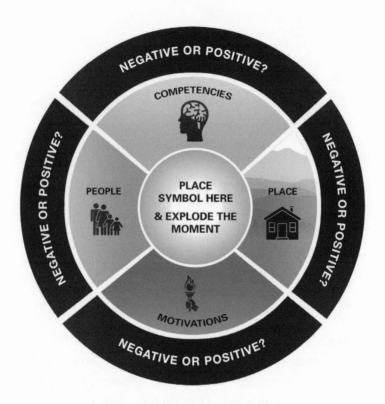

As you can see, the Story Stamp has four parts. You might imagine that there are so many different stories, so many unique events, so many personalized tellings that the variety is infinite—and you'd be right! But every one of those stories can be broken down into the same four elements:

**Competencies:** The strengths or abilities in play in someone's brain during a particular lived experience.

**Motivations:** In other words, why someone acted as they did. There can be more than one.

**People:** Others who were involved in the story.

**Place:** The setting of the experience.

Although motivations, people, and place are self-explanatory, competencies can use a bit more explanation.

## COMPETENCIES

Your brain is like your central processing unit. At different times, it uses different strengths, abilities, specialties, competencies. You can call them what you like, but I call them mental muscles. Like your physical muscles, they all work in essentially the same way to achieve a task, but also like your physical muscles, different mental muscles are used for different tasks.

The brain is infinitely varied, of course, but to keep things straightforward, I divide the mental muscles into eight competencies. As was pointed out by my friend Roy Horan who was conducting research at Hong Kong Polytechnic University, the competencies can be seen as opposing pairs (although in reality they're often more like two ends of a continuum):

**Leadership/Receptivity:** Leadership is the capacity to influence others and to guide yourself. Its opposite, receptivity, includes empathy, openness, and contextual awareness.

**Adaptability/Discrimination:** Adaptability is letting go, being suitably flexible, maintaining balance, and adjusting to change. The contrast is discrimination, which is being analytical, seeing fine details, and making distinctions, which can prevent flexibility.

**Communication/Organization:** Communication is exchanging ideas and being able to package a message to an intended audience. It's different from organization because it's external and interpersonal, whereas organization is internal. Organization is how things work together, a schedule, a business, a team, a project—or an economy.

**Exploration/Creativity:** Exploration is research; it's getting out of your comfort zone and wandering or thinking without planning. Creativity, on the other hand, is making something, like creating an itinerary for your actions. It is putting something new into existence.

At any point in time, your mental muscles are connected to what's happening in your world—and you can match them to one or several of these eight competencies. The Story Stamp helps you pin down which, together with the other elements of the story.

## USING THE STORY STAMP

Have you ever heard anyone say something like this: "Oh, it was not a good time in my life, but I managed through it"?

It's pessimistic language. It also doesn't convey anything about the speaker, never mind now communicating anything of positive value about the speaker to the outside world. What does it mean, you "managed through it"? What happened? Did you let go and become adaptable? Or did you start to communicate with influence, which is communication and leadership?

Once you start to think about an experience using specific language, you can become more technical about dissecting the lived experience and its contribution to your life.

It's the same with motivation. It could be money, status, or a need for attention. It could be that something was required of you. Or that you took responsibility for something because your sense of duty or internal values told you it was the right thing to do. These motivations are all slightly different.

People and place add context and color. Who else was involved? Was it family, friends, or coworkers? A large group of people or just one or two? And where did the experience take place? Was it inside or outside? Somewhere enclosed such as a room or somewhere more open, by the ocean, in the mountains, or in the desert? Was it in a schoolyard or on a basketball court?

The Story Stamp is designed to help us break things down with precision. The more technical we can be, the more value we can unpack from our blue dot and the more we can do with it as we build our PeakStory.

## FIRST-DAY BLUES

Take a story from when I was a kid, in fact from my first day at school. I was excited to start school, but it turned out that I had been put in a class of non-English-speaking kids, I guess on account of having a Portuguese surname. In fact, my Portuguese was very poor (it still is—just ask my grandmother). My name made people assume I didn't speak English. I spoke it well enough to understand when the teacher spoke negatively about Portuguese American people. *My* people. She thought I didn't know what she was saying.

That took away the excitement. It was confusing and hurtful. So now that was a negative experience.

I didn't want to seem upset. I didn't want to let this get in the way of my first learning experience. After all, she was going to be my teacher for the year. So there's my motivation right there. If anything, I became more eager to learn.

In terms of competencies, I guess I turned down my leadership but turned up the analytical, understanding why it happened, and also exploration so that I became focused on learning in order to show that I belonged.

How about people? Well, teachers were around, of course, plus my parents and many family elders. That might be why I was so upset at the teacher's criticism of Portuguese Americans because I was surrounded by them. As for place, I guess that would be the school or even the specific class.

### POSITIVE/NEGATIVE

Look again at the Story Stamp. It has an outer ring surrounding the four slices of the central pie. This outer part of the stamp is labeled negative or positive because at any one time, any of the four ingredients of the experience could be either. It's basically a way to figure out whether something brought you energy or took energy away.

So you could say that pushing back against a teacher's prejudice at school was half-negative because it was hurtful and I shouldn't have had to do it. But then, it was also half-positive because it made me more eager to learn than ever. I even started to help the Portuguese kids who spoke English far worse than me. So the experience turned out to be positive, even though what actually happened was negative.

As you use the Story Stamp, maybe you realize that a person was negative but an experience was positive, say, because you were able to use your openness and receptivity to identify that somebody was being picked on, and you had the courage to voice that that wasn't an appropriate way to treat another human being.

So that was the birthplace of your warrior-caregiver persona, or your heroic-caregiver, or your defender of what's good in human beings. Maybe it's a clue that helps you start to see the genesis of a theme in your story. And isn't that better than "Oh, it was not a good time in my life, but I managed through it"?

But this is only one experience, so don't get carried away, people. We don't know where this story is going even though you've already lived it, because there's a subtext to what you've lived so far and you have not done all of the investigatory work.

I say again, this is the real Discovery Channel. This is the real National Geographic. We're going into the wild—an inside adventure.

You're going to be an objective observer. You're going to use your feelings and what you know about yourself, but the Story Stamp will also help you get more technical. That will make you a better story creator and, eventually, a better performer.

One word of warning. Not all dots might be blue dots for your PeakStory. The Story Stamp helps you decide whether you really grabbed a blue dot or not. Say you loved surfing as a kid or fishing. That's great, but it's a zone of activity, not a blue dot. A blue dot is a formative experience, a specific moment in time.

Be sure to land on a blue dot, not a zone of your life. We want to know one particular moment within any activity that stands out and why that might be.

## THE PHENOMENOLOGY PHENOMENON

This kind of studying your mind through subjective lived experiences comes from the phenomenological method figured out by my mentor in grad school, Dr. Amedeo Giorgi. The more I used it, the more I realized that everybody could use its tools to gather data to understand their own life. It enables you to think about yourself with rigor. But you don't have to go and get a PhD to understand it.

Phenomenology helps anyone stake a claim to the elements of an experience. Anyone can reverse engineer an experience and study it in a similar way as a trained phenomenologist or social scientist. You don't have to be a professor who published in an academic journal to benefit from phenomenology.

You can unzip the backpack of experiences you've been filling all your life, let it fall on the ground, and unpack the goodies. You can pick through and find the competencies or mental muscles, the motivations, the power of place or of people. You get to say, "Okay, I had some good stuff going on here. Here's why I did it. Here's how I did it. Here's who was around when those things happened. Here's why the place mattered."

## RETURNING TO MOMENTS

All activities happen in a physical space or place. People make decisions based on place. Maybe they have a suspicion that they don't want to be in office buildings, or they want to be out west. I suspect that if they went through a reflective practice, they could probably trace back that desire to be out in nature to enjoying playing outdoors as a kid, or maybe to being denied that chance, so they want to give it to their children.

You know this to be true. You've returned to different things in your life. Everyone does. Why do people buy old cars and relive the experience of being with Dad in the 1969 T-Bird or the 1974 Alfa Romeo?

Why do people gather and tell stories about what they experienced? Partly because those were important moments in their lives *then*. When they were with friends or maybe driving and talking or sharing political ideas or discussing what was happening in the world. But also because telling their stories helps them belong *now*, because others recognize stories in their own lives with a similar vibe, energy, or essence.

There are reasons why we go to extremes at times to collect and resurrect old cars, old watches, vintage clothes. It's a sort of unconscious nostalgia. And by analyzing it, we're making the unconscious conscious to the extent that we spend real time thinking about it—and telling stories about it.

## NEUTRAL SPACE

When you start to use the Story Stamp, it's critical to find yourself a space with some neutrality. People tell me they put music on that has no lyrics or take a walk with their PeakStory journal so they can take notes. Even though we have digital tools and online courses, people find this offline time very powerful.

Remember Marshall Davis Jones and his poem about being overconnected and underrelated? We need to be able to unplug. Sometimes you'll just find a corner in your office or change chairs. But you need to make space.

I know this is technical, but it's also fun. It's like watching detective shows. We're curious about what the investigators will discover. We love exploration, watching it or doing it. That's what you're doing. You're tapping into one of the universal competencies that every human being has: exploration.

The Story Stamp is the framework you use to decode your experiences. It's influenced by the literature from academic studies. The organized methodology is there to help you create a story through analysis. The method has helped some *Fortune* 500 company leaders, it's helped business development experts, academics, and entrepreneurs—and it can help you, too, so open yourself up.

## A FAMOUS PEAKSTORY

After I'd constructed the PeakStory method, I became aware of how the best speeches incidentally validated it. One of the best examples was the Stanford Commencement Speech given by the late Steve Jobs, then the CEO of Apple Computer and Pixar Animation, on June 12, 2005.

Jobs literally said, the first story is about connecting the dots.

Oftentimes, we use that phrase, but we don't appreciate what it means. For some people, it suggests randomness. In fact, we're derandomizing, as we are here.

Look at Jobs's transcript here (https://news.stanford. edu/2005/06/14/jobs-061505/) or watch his video. You'll find the hero story, the collaborative story, and the virtuous story without any help.

The first story Jobs tells is about dropping out of Reed College after six months. He stayed around for another eighteen months because what he really wanted to do was drop into classes that he found fascinating versus being in classes that didn't really mean anything to him. This was heroic because when Jobs was adopted as a young child, his biological mother made his adopted parents promise he would someday go to college, which neither of them had done. That was a requirement before she would sign the adoption papers.

Seventeen years later, not only is he in college, but he has also naively chosen to go to a college that is almost as expensive as Stanford. It cost nearly all of his working-class parents' savings, but they were going to honor their commitment. Imagine the pressure on him; being heroic for him was staying in college, so as not to blow his mother's and father's hard-earned money. But he couldn't see the value in college, so he didn't know what he was going to do. He stayed but did college differently. He opened up his receptivity and exploration and began discovering.

And he was pretty scared and he was broke. He slept on the floors of friends' rooms. He returned Coke bottles for five-cent deposits to buy food. He would walk seven miles across town every Sunday to get a free meal at the Hare Krishna spiritual center.

Eventually, he stumbled into a calligraphy class, and he got interested. He learned about typefaces and about varying the amount of space between letter combinations. It didn't seem like it had any application in his life, but ten years later, when he was designing the first Apple personal computer, the connection was made. He changed the way computer fonts look and came up with the first computer with beautiful typography.

Jobs's collaborative story happened when he started Apple in the garage with Steve Wozniak. A decade later, it became a $2 billion company. Then there was a negative collaborative moment when he got fired from Apple. But, in fact, it was the best thing that ever happened to him because, in his words, the heaviness of being successful was replaced by the lightness of being a beginner again.

The virtuous moment was starting another company. That company, Pixar, went on to create the world's first computer animated feature. Maybe you've heard of it: *Toy Story*. It's now the most successful story in the world. In a remarkable turn of events, Jobs then returned to Apple, where the technology he developed is still at the heart of the company's renaissance.

Jobs's speech connects more dots, but those are the ones that mattered most. He goes on to talk about having cancer. By then, he had figured out years earlier that if you live each day as if it were the last, then someday, it will be. So for thirty-three years, he would look at the mirror and ask himself, "Is this what I want to do today?"

Whenever the answer was no for too many days, he would know that he needed to change.

## A PURPOSEFUL LIFE

When I stumbled across this speech, I actually shed a tear because it was such a beautiful validation of the PeakStory method. (Yes, that was a blue dot for me!) Jobs was so obviously connecting blue dots to create the arc of his life story. And he showed who he really was, which was not just this ruthless business guy but a pioneer-explorer. A creator and explorer who went into unchartered territories over and over again, then eventually became settled in the way that exploration gets you into areas where you also see opportunity.

So when Jobs gave this speech, he was already six months over his life expectancy from the doctors' prognosis. He was thinking about his own existence very differently because he had death on the doorstep. But the speech is not about dying. It is about living a meaningful, purposeful life—even though his life looked very disconnected at one point.

So let's get to living by getting to discovering and leveraging these tools in your own life. It's almost like a call to get to work.

## CHANGING GOALS

You may start to see the light at this point in the method. You're about to use these tools to find those moments and dust them off. To be an archaeologist in your life. Sometimes the dig looks bigger than it is, but don't worry. The thing is probably right below the surface. This is not therapy, although I have been told it can be therapeutic. When you tell your story, you will feel more whole, as if the Vaseline was suddenly removed from your eyeglasses. You can see your path.

Remember that your peak is always changing. Nothing is final. The process has continuity built in.

It's like exercising. Your first goal might be to run a mile, but when you get there, you raise it to two, to three, whatever. Lo and behold, you're at your new peak. So think about this as an ongoing process. You're going to continue to live, you're going to collect more dots. Some will be blue, some not.

The blue dots may change as you're going through the method. You will remember different blue dots in your past, perhaps adding some and deleting others, but the target doesn't move that much because it's always based in your life today.

So will you encounter more blue dots in your life? Yes. Formative things can still happen, regardless of age. And when they do, now you have a method to interpret them. You'll start to look at your life with a heightened consciousness, and if something happens that has blue-dot qualities, add it to your PeakStory map.

## EXERCISE: THE STORY STAMP

You've learned about the Story Stamp. Now it's your turn.

Revisit the nine blue dots you found from the last exercise: three hero, three collaborative, three virtuous and choose one per level.

You're going to Story Stamp each one of those to find out what richness it holds.

We're going small to go big. We'll get into the details that will ensure that your overarching story begins to come together.

As we move on with the method, you might decide that one of your original dots isn't quite as satisfying as you'd want it to be. No problem. Just go back and Story Stamp one of the other dots from the same level.

But know that to start with, you don't have to do all nine dots.

When you choose your first dot, which will be a hero story, think about what the experience means. Why do you suspect it stood out to you? What is its significance? Write it in your journal. Like the police say on TV shows, if you recall any detail, no matter how small, make a note.

Then work through the dot again. This time, use the Story Stamp model. Use your journal to break the experience down into competencies, motivations, people, and place.

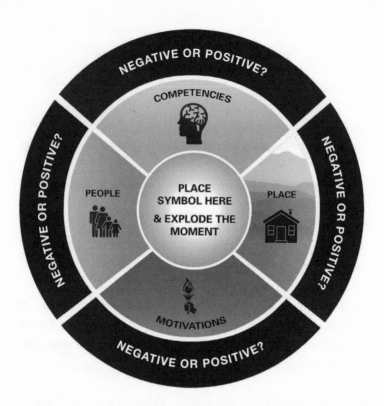

Compare the two interpretations of the moment. What do you learn from using the Story Stamp?

Now go on and Story Stamp a collaborative dot and a virtuous dot. Note the details in your story journal. They're the details that provide the texture and vibrancies of the experiences in your PeakStory.

# CHAPTER 6

---

# THEMES AND THREADS

*"If knowing yourself and being yourself were as easy to do as to talk about, there wouldn't be nearly so many people walking around in borrowed postures, spouting secondhand ideas, trying desperately to fit in rather than to stand out."*
—WARREN G. BENNIS, *ON BECOMING A LEADER*

The Story Stamp expands blue-dot moments to draw out microdetails of those experiences: the competencies, motivations, people, and places. We went small so that we could really unpack meaning. Magnifying-glass small. But we were going small so that we could eventually go big.

Themes and threads link our dots together. They help us pick out patterns. They're not always obvious, but if we can tease them out, they help in two ways: they shape our story and they tell us something about ourselves.

It's like when you're choosing a movie or a book. On Netflix or Prime, the movies are categorized by genres. In a bookstore or a library, the books are also arranged by genre, fiction here, romances there, detectives, thrillers, horror.

We categorize just about everything we encounter because it reflects how humans think. We see patterns, similarities, groups.

And you see aspects of yourself over time in the same way. So what's your story? Is it a drama? Is it a drama-comedy? Are you maybe Will Smith in *The Pursuit of Happyness*, and you're a protector-provider, just like Chris Gardner, the real-life character he plays in the movie? Early in his career, Gardner struggled with homelessness while he looked after his young son and started what turned out to be a highly successful career in stockbroking.

## GENERIC THINKING

The way we sort ourselves into genres is by going small to go big. There's not always a theme that stands out, so at first, we start with the details and bring them together and see if a thread emerges.

Look out for threads that run through your blue dots. Perhaps you were always a teacher because you helped a kid in class who was having trouble reading or doing math. Or maybe there was a classmate who was a bit of an outcast socially, and you found the language to bring her or him into a conversation. Maybe you were a caregiver, so that might be a theme to look for in your other dots.

I'm going to give you some language that's a bit like a magic code. It's going to trigger things you already know, and you're going to get excited about it. You're going to get excited because it's super affirming. And from the affirmation, you're going to start to grow in confidence that your story over time makes sense. That there is integration and cohesion. The dots belong together.

I once had a video crew at our home in southern Rhode Island, capturing the video companion to this book, which I was then using in a university class. The house is in the woods but also close to the ocean. To explain how themes and threads work when building a PeakStory, I showed them a vine growing up in an oak tree. And I said, "You can see that there's this commonality. The leaves don't turn into different leaves. They vary in color and the line changes as the vine grows, but they don't become a different sort of leaf. They're vine leaves." The same holds true of a theme. It remains constant.

So in your PeakStory, we want to see the same continuity. We want to see threads and themes running through because that shows the stability to the core of who you are.

## THE FOURSQUARE

Even though you're going to go big in terms of identifying themes and threads, we still have to go small again, then switch back and forth. When you look at the ingredients (going small), you'll eventually be able to see the themes and threads (going big). To help you along, we're going to use what I call the *Foursquare*. The Foursquare is a way to look at your three hero experiences, three collaborative moments, and three virtuous moments and pull out the competencies or mental muscles, the motivation, the people, and the place.

I call it the Foursquare because you can just write it out in a big square divided into four boxes of equal size. In the middle, draw a circle that includes part of each box, like a bull's-eye.

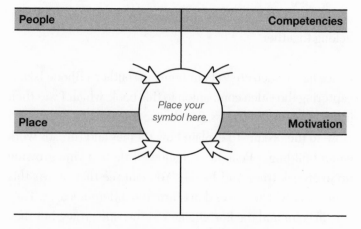

| People | | Competencies |
| --- | --- | --- |
| | *Place your symbol here.* | |
| Place | | Motivation |

Label the first box competency and list all the competencies from each blue-dot moment. Label the remaining three boxes motivations, people, and place and list those in the respective boxes. As you distribute the attributes from each blue dot into the appropriate boxes, look for repetition, words that come up two, three, six, or eight times.

Move those into the bull's-eye, or use arrows to point them there. It's also possible to place a single symbol there that brings together all the qualities you are gathering. We'll look into this more closely in the exercise at the end of the chapter.

## MY FOURSQUARE

For me, the competencies would be creativity, being a deep listener and an explorer, and also an analyzer of details. I get stuff right. And knowing it all works together well means that my motivation is to give someone a tool. I could see people were disengaged from their work and it spilled over to their home life and their ability to control their emotions, and I also wanted to democratize learning tools that were usually reserved for executive development so people could be more engaged and happy. I've always been doing that sort of thing, from my hero story to my collaborative story through to my virtuous moment.

When we start to think about particular kinds of people, for me, it was always students, even in corporate America, or coaching, or at the university. I would always teach.

As you fill in the Foursquare, you'll start to see the theme running through your life. It's no surprise that the theme for me was *very* teacher-y, *very* professorial but inclusive, with a for-everyone vibe or feeling.

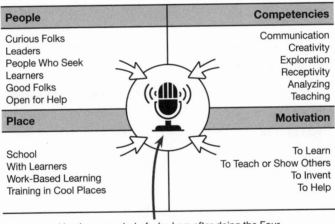

| People | Competencies |
|--------|--------------|
| Curious Folks | Communication |
| Leaders | Creativity |
| People Who Seek | Exploration |
| Learners | Receptivity |
| Good Folks | Analyzing |
| Open for Help | Teaching |
| **Place** | **Motivation** |
| School | To Learn |
| With Learners | To Teach or Show Others |
| Work-Based Learning | To Invent |
| Training in Cool Places | To Help |

Here's my symbol of who I am after doing the Four Square Exercise. What's your symbol?

The symbol in the center of my Foursquare is an old-school microphone, the kind the principal uses to address the school, as often seen in the movies. Why did I pick this symbol? Because when I looked at all of the information the Foursquare collects from my blue dots after I Story Stamped them, it was clear to me that my goals moving forward are linked to helping others build their story, then voice it.

## IDENTIFYING PATTERNS

The Foursquare is a very simple methodology for breaking down your experiences and consolidating your dots. You'll try it for yourself in the exercise at the end of the chapter.

Your job is to recognize patterns. Is there commonality or consistency of beliefs? Do you see similarities between things? Are you seeing things that you're letting go of—that is, are you being flexible when you need to be? Do you see things that you're adhering to more or doing with more frequency or depth? Maybe you were a caregiver by mistake, but you've reclaimed the role in the middle of your life and you really want to manifest it on the virtuous level as a leader-caregiver. How can you do that in your current role?

## POWER OF ARCHETYPES

One way to think about the patterns you find is to imagine that you're emerging as a character in a book or movie. How do you fashion yourself as this character?

George Lucas, the movie director, relied on archetypes, or stock figures that represent a particular type of person. In particular, he was inspired by the myth scholar Joseph Campbell, author of *A Hero with a Thousand Faces*, and built a movie that was kind of a hit: *Star Wars*.

From studying myths around the world, Campbell came up with the idea that although there were seemingly countless types of individuals, there are also particular structures for their stories that convey their journeys with more impact. Even though many archetypes exist, he was particularly fascinated by the hero archetype. Lucas clearly realized that we can relate to those archetypes in a movie if their emerging hero narratives unfold in a precise manner. Lucas also learned from Campbell that although myths seem to take place externally, they also take place within us, in what Campbell calls "the outer reaches of inner space."

In the first half of the 1900s, the Austrian psychologist Carl Jung studied where archetypes come from. He proposed that archetypal characters are a counterpoint of instinct that come from our collective unconscious. Now Jungian psychologists suggest that we can all relate to what became known as the twelve Jungian archetypes: innocent, everyman, hero, outlaw, explorer, creator, ruler, magician, lover, caregiver, jester, and sage. When you look at these roles, even if you're not a psychologist, you can recognize them in others and in yourself. Teachers are often sages, while everyone has a period without experiences when they're innocent.

Carol Pearson, who's a contemporary Jungian psychologist, references archetypes in connection with brands. In *The Hero and Outlaw*, which she wrote with Margaret Mark, she investigated particularly how brands can connect with certain archetypes. What Jung started years ago continues to influence Pearson's identification of, for example, six heroic archetypes: the orphan, the wanderer, the innocent, the magician, the warrior, and the altruist.

Your audience contains the same archetypes, so they recognize them and relate to them. Archetypes are ways to understand and project ourselves because we all have common archetypes. Everybody is a caregiver. Everybody has innocence. Everybody can be everybody.

## NEW LANGUAGE

I know I'm going a little wild on you with all this content. I can't help it: I'm a professor who teaches psychology, leadership, and public speaking, too! But the notion of themes and threads is vital to understand that we're trying to introduce new language to describe how your character will be seen in the movie of your life.

Archetypes provide the language.

Are you a little more like a magician-creator, or are you a little bit like a compliance auditor? Are you more of an innocent, or are you more of a caregiver? Are you more of a jester, a creator, or a teacher? Are you more like a ruler or more like a sage like Yoda?

Are you a caregiver at all costs? Are you a converter who converts things? A puzzle solver? An obstacle obliterator? Are you a tireless advocate for social justice? Are you an individual who builds community?

I once had an executive leadership client who as a young kid used to create plays and shows by enlisting people in her neighborhood. She could spot talent and knew how to engage people and where they belonged in the show. She then became a major event coordinator but is now the Chief Operating Officer in a successful company. We looked at her themes, and she identified an archetype, organizer-helper, where she was always coordinating events and processes to engage people. Her engagement shaped the workplace culture. In many ways, she's still producing plays, much like when she was a kid. These days, however, instead of an audience of parents watching the plays, it's about the workers, employees, and leaders feeling good about the performance of work.

My client went small to go big. When she zoomed out of her details, she saw a theme of being an engager of talent in fun ways from the neighborhood to current corporate life. Everything she did was about creating a culture that feels right. She realized that she always had a knack for adding life to the dull and humdrum. Now, as a chief, she could really use her leadership to build cultures for meaning-making work. Great stuff.

I hear she's thinking about writing a book now, *The Production of Culture*. No doubt, it's a nod to her story of becoming who she is and how she now helps others build workplace cultures with that neighborhood vibe!

## CONNECTION THROUGH TIME

A theme or thread connects the chapters of your life over time—like the vine connects the leaves. Your narrative takes place over time, making it a critical element of the stories that make up your narrative. Stories on their own retell one moment. Your hero story is from the past. Your collaborative moment might be from the near now, but it is probably an imagined variation of the future you.

Don't worry if you haven't had a full virtuous experience yet, perhaps because you're younger or you're not yet in the right company in the right position. You don't need to have a virtuous experience fully formed at the moment: maybe you've just sniffed it, like the aroma of a good cup of coffee. But now's the time that you'll build an imagined likely version of your future out of that virtuous moment—whether it's partly or fully realized, or whether you need to fill it out yourself.

The language of archetypes will help you understand the role you're playing now and the role you aspire to fill in your virtuous moment.

I had a student who agreed to be an example to the class of the PeakStory method. We created her PeakStory map, applied the Story Stamp to her blue dots, and then filled in a Foursquare. I asked the class to think of the superhero the student would be.

Without hesitation, they said, "She's Wonder Woman."

When I asked them why, they said their classmate uses her qualities of power and regality to ricochet and deflect negativity in her life. Everything she does deflects negativity. She does it to protect her three kids. She does it to be an advocate in her job. And she was doing it by being an advocate for herself by going back to school.

This was self-affirming to the student, who just stood there at the whiteboard and then said, "Wow, I'm a modern Wonder Woman."

## LIFE AND THE MOVIES

If you get stuck trying to associate an archetype with your blue dots, one thing you can do is ask somebody else, "Say, these are some key moments in my life. What kind of character do you think I am? If you were to pick someone from a movie, a superhero or a classic movie, or a film or a book, who would it be?"

I get it if you don't have anyone to ask or you don't want to ask someone else. Most people like to keep this stage as an inside job. And guess what? You have the answer anyway. Whatever your answer is, you're guaranteed to be right!

Look for the themes that emerge from your dots. What do you perceive about your essence, which all these experiences form together? The evidence from the small details of your blue dots animates you into this big space where your character finally becomes apparent.

Are you like a superhero? Wonder Woman? Black Panther? Superman? Are you more like Woody from *Toy Story*? What character in a movie are you similar to or in a book you read? Maybe you're like Violet the invisible girl from the *Incredibles* movie, where you quietly observe everything without being seen, but then you appear and save the day. You're someone with keen receptivity who absorbs and remembers details and can step up to lead when necessary.

When we think about characters within a genre, the archetypes within that genre comes to mind. Genres and archetypes help you see themes that are familiar and follow patterns. And our brains like to think in patterns.

## CREATING ROLES

I've thrown a lot of language at you, but this type of language—teacher or caregiver, leader or explorer, sage or magician, and so on—helps generate an understanding of a theme that develops over time. The Foursquare allows you to sort the small to get to the big. Then we can start creating archetypes based on competencies and motivations to describe the type of person you are. Although different psychologists identify different archetypes, we can choose our own. Each of us has more than one archetype within. You can combine them to name your personal archetype. I'll give you some possibilities that come from students in class. Maybe you'll grab one or two you can use in your PeakStory:

- Heroic caregiver
- Gentle caregiver
- Achiever producer
- Purposeful caregiver
- Tireless advocate
- Creative teacher
- Positively challenging partner
- Loyal producer
- Catalyst to change
- Empathetic counselor
- Practical artist
- Pioneer quester
- Adapting to give
- Dutiful soldier
- Leader with a heart
- Teacher explorer
- Leader learner
- Perfectionistic for a good cause
- Humble producer
- Quiet contemplator
- Thinker then doer

You can always create more combinations of these words to define you than what I provided above. Or you can even add new words or word combinations that may characterize you.

## GONE TO THE DOGS

I love dogs, so I'm going to give you an analogy for archetypes using dogs. (If you're not a dog person, pretend we're talking about cats.)

When you see a dog, you don't see a random animal. You see a dog. And you don't see the cells that make it up. You see the dog, and you don't just see a dog; you see a type of dog. It appears to you as an Australian shepherd, a boxer, a labradoodle, a designer dog, a mutt. But they're all dogs.

They're all the same, but they're all different. I think that's a good way to understand what Jung was getting at with archetypes. All people are people, just with some emerging characteristics more likely to be rising as they play, work, and be. Just like dogs.

If it helps establish how archetypes work, try thinking about yourself as a dog for a while. Play with that idea. Maybe that'll spark the kind of person you're becoming. Are you a guard dog, a playful dog, a faithful companion, an aggressive protector? Dogs are all different, but different breeds have certain traits that characterize them.

Does that help think about what kind of person you are? Look at the details. Go small to go big. What kind of manifestation of those traits turns into your character archetype?

Once you've moved from the small to the big, you can start to put your story together with even more energy and more confidence. And that's what the next chapter is about.

## EXERCISE: USING THE FOURSQUARE

A key element of your PeakStory is time. A theme that is consistent over time reveals an undeniable truth that something excites you in particular situations, even if all the elements might not be perfect.

Remember, this is the real Discovery Channel. It's real science because you're gathering evidence of consistency over time. You're learning about yourself analytically.

We're looking for consistency so we can string it all together.

You already have the answers. They're somewhere in the elements of the Story Stamp.

To identify your patterns, start by creating a Foursquare. Take a horizontal sheet of paper or journal page (I sometimes write it on the window with a whiteboard marker) and use a ruler to divide it into quarters. In the middle, put a big circle like a bull's-eye.

Now label your four sections with the qualities from the Story Stamp exercise. The upper right is competencies, the bottom right is motivations, the lower left is place, and the top left is people. (The bull's-eye is empty for now.)

Now look back at the dots you Story Stamped. Write down the competencies, motivations, people, and places from each in the appropriate box.

Look for patterns. Maybe some competencies appear three times because they showed up across all three dots, such as communication. Maybe you see that all your dots took place out of doors. I had a client who changed her work pattern because she realized she wanted to spend more time outdoors, communicating and leading.

You're likely firing off different competencies in the hero (past), the collaborative (near now or past), and the virtuous (future possible). If you're outdoors a lot, draw an arrow to the bull's-eye; if you're always influencing a group of people, draw that arrow to the bull's-eye.

Use arrows to link all the important words into the bull's-eye.

What about the power of place? Do you prefer a pressured environment or somewhere more calm?

Again, pull the important words or themes into the bull's-eye.

When you've looked at all four sections, look at the bull's-eye. The elements that have made it here create a central connection across the chapters of your life. Now think of a symbol that sums up that connection. Draw this symbol in the middle of the bull's-eye. For me, it's an old-school microphone because I'm a teacher, but also because I teach people how to speak. For others, it might be an ear because they're a good listener. One student drew a fan. When I asked why, they said, "Because I cool people down." Another person put a stopwatch because they could organize anything quickly.

Keep your Foursquare in your story journal. If you've written it somewhere else, take a photo and paste it into your book.

It's the basis of your PeakStory.

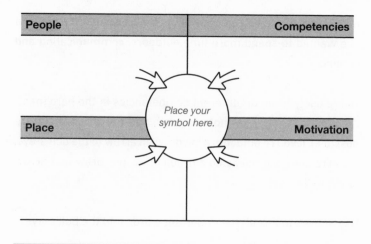

# CHAPTER 7

―――――

# CREATING YOUR PEAKSTORY

*"Life can only be understood backwards; but it must be lived forwards."*

—Søren Kierkegaard

It's time to create your PeakStory. Before we're ready, however, we need to sort our building blocks, the blue dots.

Everything starts from Bluedot-ville.

Remember Steve Jobs and his famous commencement speech at Stanford in 2005? His story was informed and transformed by everything he experienced, including dropping in on calligraphy classes at Reed College, which might seem to have nothing to do with leading a technology company but has everything to do with the storypath of his life.

So how did he decide on his blue dots? He sorted them.

The dots Jobs used are just some of the many possible dots he could have used. Like you and me—like everyone who has a lived life—he was a serial blue-dot collector. Everyone has so many, but we've used the PeakStory map to narrow yours down to the nine that seem strongest, the ones that stand out.

So now you're going to be sorting.

We're going back to the Story Stamp and the Foursquare.

## STORY SORTING

Use the storypathing table as your story sorting worksheet to bring your blue dots together.

# StoryPathing™

**PeakStorytelling™ Story Crafting Worksheet**

Intention: _____

Where will your story be told?

_____

Who will your audience be? _____

Time of Day: _____

What are some special details about your audience that might be important to consider?

_____

_____

This StorySorting™ Table can help you decide which elements to include in your PeakStorytelling™ speech or conversational exchange. Use it to sort story elements. Note your motive to include each part.

|  | HERO | COLLABORATIVE | VIRTUOUS |
|---|---|---|---|
| FE #1 |  |  |  |
| Why might you include it? |  |  |  |
| Highlighted competencies/skills: |  |  |  |
| FE #2 |  |  |  |
| Why might you include it? |  |  |  |
| Highlighted competencies/skills: |  |  |  |
| FE #3 |  |  |  |
| Why might you include it? |  |  |  |
| Highlighted competencies/skills: |  |  |  |

Note the three columns with the headings hero, collaborative, and virtuous.

Take a hero blue dot, or formative experience, and write it in the first row of the hero column. Do the same for a collaborative experience, writing it in the second column, and a virtuous experience for the third.

Then go back to your hero experience in column one, and on the second row, explain why you might include that blue dot in your story. What would it contribute? Maybe the artwork competition you won in seventh grade showed an aptitude for being an artist, even though no one thought of you as one, but it was also competitive and creative. Maybe switching colleges showed that you were more of an independent thinker than anyone knew.

You can draw the table in your journal or create a spreadsheet. As you explore each experience, fill in the boxes. It might seem like a chore, but trust me, it helps to write it down.

Each time you write down a formative experience, ask yourself, "Why might I include it?" Refer to the Story Stamp for each blue dot and your Foursquare to consider the competency or competencies that are highlighted. Is the motivation clear? Make a note in the next row. (Don't worry too much about going into the power of people or place. They'll naturally show up in your description of the experience.)

## NINE-DOT MENU

By the time you complete the table, you'll have a menu of nine dots. You've condensed the experiences, you've explained why you might include them, and you've listed the competencies and motivations they highlight.

Well, hello. As always, me search is the best research. Now we're in business. Now we're ready to build your story.

So what do you do? You've got all of this information that you can study, but it looks overwhelming. No cause for alarm. The key is that you're not going to use all nine dots.

This is the story of three dots. A hero dot, a collaborative dot, and a virtuous dot is all it takes to anchor you in the past to show how you've become the person you are today and will become in the near future.

## WHAT'S YOUR INTENTION?

The key question to help select your dots is this: What's your intention with this story? What do you want to achieve?

If you're going to tell it to yourself, perhaps it's to be clear about who you really are, to help with decisions you're making about school—yes, storypathing and the PeakStory method help you rewrite the stories you tell yourself. Pretty neat, huh? If you're telling it to others, it might be to establish your credibility or reputation as a new leader or to reverse the misslice. Let me remind you what I mean by misslice. People may think of you as a particular kind of person because of how you look, because of your name, or what they've heard about you through the grapevine, but you want to counter that misslice.

The listener wants to know how you came to be the person you are, and you want to tell them. You have a hero dot that anchors you by showing that you can overcome obstacles en route to working with others. And a collaborative dot that shows you're not just this strong hero who battles obstacles all day. You spiral up in the PeakStory map to an area where you're with others at work and in life and recreationally, doing this wonderful work that you love. You show them you're an obstacle overcomer whom they might want to work with because they hear that you're collaborative. And that through your collaboration, you're heading toward this peak in your PeakStory, which is your virtuous moment.

That's how to counter the misslice. But to make it work, we've got to build those thoughts out. It looks easy in this example, but how do *you* tell that story? You have to decide the pieces to include and craft your message.

## AUDIENCE ANALYSIS

The hero dot you choose to begin your story depends on whom you're talking to, so let's do a bit of audience analysis.

Who's listening to your story and where? Maybe you're at a conference with peers in the financial sector. Or is the audience a mix of leaders, middle managers, and new inductees? Will someone else introduce you? Or are you in a casual setting in the pub? Is this a real meeting or a Zoom video call? You can see the power of place and people work together.

Your intention in telling your story and your audience analysis will guide which dot you're selecting and why, and also how much of the dot that you unveil. Remember, we can always flatten the dot to fit the story embodied by you, the storyteller. The dots show you have worth and value, so we flip the pattern and flatten or condense the dots to show your positive attributes.

Don't forget that, folks.

You're in control and you're ready. As you're telling your story to this audience, don't worry if something goes a bit left or right because you always know what your core story is. That doesn't alter the individual telling you choose, which is shaped by the circumstances. If you feel yourself going off kilter, just fall back on the core story. What is the core story? It's your minimum viable story. Your MVS. The story most likely to work in all situations.

But we're not going to get into the storytelling applications and performance applications yet. We're at the build phase.

Consider the audience. What kind of people are they? Are they more spiritual, more analytical? Do they have a service background? Are they practical? Can the story you're forming now be told across varied audiences? Invariably the answer is most certainly yes—so even though crafting your story isn't a one-and-done task, you can use the same story more than once. Were you wondering about that?

## ADJUST YOUR STORY

Be reverent to your blue-dot choices. You want to tell the story that best represents your narrative identity, who you've become through your story of life, the life span arc of these three moments: hero (past), collaborative (near now or now), and virtuous (near now or likely future). Once you have your core story, it can be adjusted or contextualized for different audiences. You can shape it into a particular environment.

You use the story sorting table to think about where and when your story will be told. What is the time of day? Are there special details? The answers will help you decide which elements to include in your PeakStorytelling, whether it's for a conversational exchange, a self-introduction, or a business-development moment where you're building a client relationship.

Once you've sorted and labeled the story elements, such as motives and competencies, consider the details to include. Remember what you found out about the blue dots and about the themes and threads of your story. Now you're at a point where you can look at a blue dot and say, "This is the moment. This is the competency. This is why it must be included."

Then ask yourself again: Why did you choose that blue dot? Why does that particular story stand out to you? Because you might forget. People do, all the time. People get to the first page of sorting their blue dots, and all of a sudden, they throw it out the window because it seems irrelevant and they have to start over. Stick with what you have; there's a reason those blue dots were top of your mind when you did the exercise.

## PUTTING IT ALL TOGETHER

When you've chosen your dots, I always advise people to write out all three parts together. Write it all out: hero, collaborative, virtuous. The PeakStory comes from putting it all together.

Many people actually write their PeakStory out by hand. Not on a computer, not in Word. They actually write it down and send me pictures. They say things like, "Well, I took my journal to the park, and I sat by the pond and watched the kayakers and the wind surfers and the bass fishermen. And I just kind of hung out because I needed to think and write.

And I figured, well, I might as well show you what I did and you read my writing."

So write your story somewhere you're comfortable. Wherever. Write it down. But keep it tight. A paragraph or two per story.

Use plenty of details, but be concise—don't end up with ten pages.

## TUNE YOUR VOICE

Once you've got your story down, you need to tune your voice. Test it by reading it out loud, recording it, and listening to yourself (there's a great exercise for this at the end of the chapter). Here's a checklist to consider:

Intent and Identity. What was your intent? Do you emerge as the character that you thought you would when you started selecting your three dots? Go back and check. Was it clear? How do you know? Grab a couple of highlighters to mark the parts where you're good and the parts where you don't come across as you'd like. Work on rewriting those parts that don't work as well.

Core Message. What was the core message? Look for the thread or theme. Was it clear enough to carry through the three formative experiences?

Audience Analysis. Based on your audience, what would you tweak? What would you adjust to speak to a technical audience from a nontechnical audience? Do you need to be more analytical? Are you too creative? Are there details that digress or are disruptive for the listener?

The Bend. Your story is *your* story. It's who you are, but your core story—those three favorite dots—can be bent to an audience. How are you able to bend it? I've taught inmates in prisons and the police officers who put them there. I teach executives, people in transition, and students in the classroom at Roger Williams University. My story bends all the time. Yours will, too.

Pacing. Pacing is key. Reading your story out loud is the best way to notice and correct parts of it that you feel don't really capture everything. People have a habit of speeding up when they lose their way. If that happens, why did you speed up?

Dialogical Styling. Can you see parts of your story where you could pause to let the audience engage? Not for a full dialogue—you're not exchanging views—but chances to poke at the audience or ask a rhetorical question. Set them up with an unusual link—I used to be an artist and I'm in finance now—and give them a moment to react. That sets up a dialogue.

Punctuation. You don't have to drop the mic or puff your chest out and pump your arms like some crazy person in an old-school video. But do make sure that the audience knows that the story has actually ended or is ending.

## "HOW DID YOU GET INTO FINANCE ANYWAY?"

Let me show you how different dots can be brought together that initially seem random. I'll tell you about a wealth advisor and financial planner I know whose story is the perfect response when he's in the car on the way to lunch at a conference and someone inevitably says to him, "How did you get into finance anyway?"

He brings together three dots: a journey as a kid, serving as a ship's officer, and going into finance.

"So all this came from not being afraid to travel down from Albany on the train to meet my dad in New York, where he worked, when I was just fourteen [hero story]. When Dad left his job to start his own company in the stock market, I would have never thought that I would run his business one day. I joined the US Navy, becoming an officer. One time, I was on a US Navy ship in the middle of the Indian Ocean, and I helped save the life of someone on another ship. If you've never seen two ships meeting in the middle of the ocean, it's like transferring someone out the window of the twentieth story of one high-rise to the high-rise next door. We had to fly a helicopter from our ship to the other to rescue the ailing person. And we were a military ship helping a commercial ship, so there was more risk than a training manual could ever show. But we saved the person's life [collaboration story]. When I left the US Navy, I went to work with my dad and I was successful. The business grew so much that we merged it with another practice. I love helping people create stability through the language of finance [virtuous story]."

There you go: hero, collaborative, and virtuous. All pulled from apparently different fields—but all telling the same PeakStory.

## STORY BREAKDOWN

Let's break the story down.

So it's clear from the story that one of the guy's archetypes is as a stability-generating caregiver. In addition, the story makes clear his ability to adapt through knowledge when risk is high. That serves well in financial markets as well as on a ship on the Indian Ocean. These are complex situations with multiple dynamics and randomness, so for his story to make sense, he had to emerge not just as a caregiver but as a caregiver who seeks to understand variables and who has a good organizational muscle. (I use the word "organization" as a competency, as a processing muscle that knows how things work. This is not about keeping your desk tidy; it's about being able to break down the complex to make it simple or looking at something simple and understanding its complexity.)

This financial planner could incorporate these qualities into his organizational schema to create a story that he's a code hacker for complex, dynamic scenarios. He showed that he knows how to self-navigate through apparent chaos by demonstrating his creativity, his patience, and his depth of understanding.

And by the way, he's a pilot. No wonder. And after you hear his story, you'll fly with him anywhere because you trust him, right? And if he's copiloting financial decision making with you, you trust him because his narrative, his blue dots, supports the fact that nobody flies a plane who isn't really thorough at risk analysis.

And the guy finishes telling his story in the car—"And I'm just glad to be with you all, so…All right, cool. Who's next?"—and everyone's going, "Wow." He's created a storypath. They see the arc of his life.

## TELLING YOUR STORY

The beauty of your PeakStory is that it's portable and adaptable. It hangs on the PeakStory map framework, it's sensible, and it generates an outcome. It will typically last maybe three and a half to five minutes, but it can be shrunk to a minute if you're only sort of teasing with dots and a couple of traits.

When you get really good at this, you can have a ninety-second version, a seventy-second version, or a two-and-a-half- to three-and-a half-minute version. You could do a full eighteen-minute TED Talk on your life. If someone asks.

But the ideal is typically three and a half to five minutes.

Time it by recording yourself.

Tell your PeakStory out loud, and use the record button on your smartphone or some other device. Most people prefer to do these initial reps by themselves before they get other people involved.

Then go back and listen to it. Slow-play it.

We can learn from pro athletes. The difference between a pro and an amateur is typically an obsession with performance evolution. Pros get feedback loops, and one of the best feedback loops possible is capturing and recording live action. When you go live, there's no place to hide.

When you look at a tape or film or digital recording of a baseball player swinging or someone fielding a ball, or a wide receiver catching or defensive ends doing an edge rush, you'll always see that that person is like, "Wow, I have to work on my hands" or "I've got to jump at that point." It'll be the same for you now that you're turning pro.

## PRIMARY FEEDBACK

Analyzing our own performance is our primary source of feedback.

Notice I'm not asking you to go and seek other others' opinions. Not yet. This is for you so you'll know your story back to front.

Listen critically. Where do you need to tweak your story? Where are you talking a little bit too much? Where are you lost in the details? Are you overexplaining, being heavy-handed? What are you going to do to cut that side story out? Do you speak with a tone of positivity and upbeatness? Are you switching tones when your story shifts so you're using your voice as an instrument to convey meaning?

If you're overdoing it, talk less. Try flattening the dots. Don't empty out all the information from each dot; just talk about the essentials.

For me, that's as simple as telling people I was a BMX guy, which means I was always engaged with my bike. That's five seconds. I'm an explorer and that's it. That's all I need to give you right now because a short telling is often enough on its own to upset the misslice that I'm a bow-tie-wearing professor who doesn't know other stuff. That's enough to make you think, well, maybe this dude knows more than it seems. It upsets the instant opinion you had because of my physical presence or maybe because of my role identity as a professor.

It's enough for me to say, "No, no, no. Don't be fooled. I need you to understand the full me, which is not just this misslice." Once I've said that, the BMX-guy version of me replaces the bow-tie professor version in your head. In fact, you can't get rid of the BMX version.

## GOING LIVE

Once you start to tell your story, people want to hear the synergy that comes from creating this new directionality in your life. You're bringing energy that's creative and synergistic. Everyone already knows how things have worked in their own lives. So to explain your own life, you only need to know how these dots have worked out. They're your teaching moments.

Even at this stage, you might still be thinking, Hey, can I change my dots? Of course you can because you've done all the work to get to know them. Swap them in or out. But practice your go-to core story first. It's like a pianist who practices scales every day; their fingers develop muscle memory so that when it's time to change the tune, they are nimble enough to play with ease.

Don't worry that your PeakStory will always sound the same. It's never going to sound the same because if you tune it and you're playing this thing live, you can't predict what the other person's going to say.

So you might pause and ask, have you ever been in the military? A question like that promotes dialogue. They might say, "Yeah, I was a US Navy officer, and what I realized is that I really liked systems and I like the way things work and I like order and stability." So now you know something about the audience.

Maybe you're thinking, this person's a real hero. That might make you more reluctant to share your own hero story.

Remember this: everyone loves to hear stories about people when they were younger. That's what's called the innocence, or child, archetype. That's why we like the naive character in the book or the movie, or the person who is a late bloomer; that's why a little kid will change our mood or we think a puppy is cute, because we know they represent this newness to life.

So you insert stories from your past. So going back to our US Navy finance guy, he might say this: "You know, it's sort of funny. Just the other day, I was thinking about how one of the scariest moments in my life was getting on a train in the eighties, when I was about fourteen, and going down to New York City to meet my dad, who was opening up a business there. From Albany, that's a big trip for a kid."

A hero story from your youth gets our listeners to pause and be receptive to what we're saying because they were young once, too.

## OVERCOME RESISTANCE

When you start to use your newly formed PeakStory, you might feel some resistance, but this is your life. It is not like you're making it up. All this actually happened. And if it's relevant, it's connected to what you're doing today—and so you need to honor yourself by including it. There's an arc that makes sense now. Trust yourself.

If you feel resistance, try this. When you fold your hands

together and interlace your fingers, one hangs over the top of the other: either your right thumb is hanging over the left, or vice versa. Now try it the other way.

It feels weird, right?

Well, get over it. If you hold your hand in that weird position for five, ten minutes, you get over it. You'll be fine. It just feels weird to begin with.

You haven't used the storytelling muscle in a while? Get over it and *Story Like You Mean It*. This is your life, so let's go. The more reps you do, the better it gets. It's like starting push-ups or leg raises or playing scales. It's a practice, just like story-telling. The more you do, the better you get. It's that simple.

You just have to get the story in because this is your innate way of behaving in the world. This is a human goal back from the beginning, deep within our psyche, but these days, we're facing Facebook more than we are face to face.

## YOUR STORY AND YOUR LIFE

You've organized your story in your mind. Now it makes sense.

You might notice, by the way, that you're already a little calmer as you walk around, or maybe you're realizing that you want to make some shifts in your work and you're calm about that. That's pretty common, too.

You've had a glimpse of the virtuous version of your life, and perhaps it's a bit different than where you are, even though you thought you were in a pretty good place. Maybe, as a financial advisor, I realize that I want to serve military veterans because it troubles me that they get so little support despite all the government systems at play. So as someone who has a bit more autonomy at this point in my career, I really want to do some work around pro bono planning for veterans. Or I want to launch a workshop or a nonprofit for veterans.

Of course, your PeakStory doesn't have to disrupt your life. There are also ways you can live it out that add energy and worth to the life you're living and the work you're doing. We know people want meaningful work and self-expression, so you need to be able to express yourself and do the meaningful work.

### Getting Heard

The other great part about telling your PeakStory is that people start telling it to other people. It gets amplified and more widely heard. You've gone viral in the real world. You've got some real "likes."

If you introduced yourself by saying you're a Certified Financial Planner, CFP, and you've been doing it for eighteen years, that is not a provocative story to retell. "Hey, do you know who I met? I met somebody today. He's like a CFP and he's been doing this for almost two decades. He graduated with an economics degree and an MBA."

Just like millions of other people.

How much more powerful is this? "I met a guy who was a former US Navy officer who saved this guy on a BP tanker and the guy was burned, so the officer made some calls for a helicopter, and then he leapfrogged to a fueling ship and to the tanker. And this guy started off learning from his dad. You know, as a kid he took the train all the way from Albany to Manhattan on his own to see his dad at work. Now his dad's retired, so this former US Navy guy just integrated the family firm into this larger organization up in Albany. And these folks too are focused on financials and are driven by caregiver hearts and are protectors of others."

If that doesn't represent an honorable disposition of somebody who is going to be helping you make financial decisions, I don't know what does.

But if you want to, go right ahead and tell them that you've been doing it for eighteen years and you have a CFP and an MBA—but you know by this point that that sounds pretty lame, right?

---

## EXERCISE: SHARING YOUR PEAKSTORY

When you've put together your story, record it on your smartphone or computer. Do it as many times as you like until you're happy with it.

People do this anywhere from eleven to dozens of times before they're okay with it. At first, don't even bother to film yourself until you're happier. As people get closer to thirty recordings, they get really excited about natural changes to this story. Some people pick a symbol for each dot. That helps prevent them getting too focused and stops them saying everything they wrote down.

By the way, folks, you're not going to goof it up because you've already done all the work. If you feel under pressure, tell the pressure to go pound sand.

The important thing is that when you are eventually pleased with your video, you share it with somebody you trust. Don't give them any more information. Just give them the video, and ask them to watch it and then write down three to five words that come to mind that characterize the kind of person you are.

You may be surprised at how powerful their response will be to your story.

Make a note of the words they send back in your journal. Some people stick them to the mirror. Others take a screenshot of the email or text.

Those are the positive words that people's brains associate with your PeakStory.

You can send your story to multiple people and write down all the sets of five words. Some people turn them into a word cloud. Some people have even framed it and kept it in their office and said, "This is how I tell my story." Those words are like artifacts that we can keep.

Performance is all about confidence, and confidence means *filled with trust*. Trust your stories. They're driven from within, because no one can argue with you if you're confident that they contributed to your life.

One more thing. You don't have to record your performance. You could actually do a live telling. Maybe if you're in a café or in a conversation, you can say, "Hey, I'm gonna say some things right now, and I want you to just write down three to five words that come to mind about me. You cool with that? So just the other day, I was thinking about the first time I flew in an airplane..." And then dot, dot, dot. Just tell the story.

I've seen it happen. People say, "Oh shit, that's cool." They say wonderful, glowing things.

This is by far the most transformative part of the whole Peak-Story process. People tell their story, they get the five words, and they start gushing. I don't care how confident they were or pretended to be. They smile. I've seen top executives blush in front of a bunch of juniors or in a group with students in their teens. It's the craziest thing.

We all want affirmation. Those five words show that we have value and worth. That's the whole point of the damn story.

Think about your life. When do people ever give you that kind of direct feedback? They just don't.

So this is fun.

---

# CHAPTER 8

# PHILOSOPHY FOR LIVING (BEYOND) AN ENGAGED LIFE

*"Action may not always bring happiness, but there is no happiness without action."*

—William James

I created the PeakStory model as a way to help individuals express their worth and value. It turned out also to be a useful psychological tool for a greater understanding of individuals' lives. But it's more than that, too. It can provide a way to understand the knowledge and reality that make up being alive.

A philosophy, in other words.

There's not much philosophy around today. We don't have many Platos or Aristotles. Maybe we listen to sports stars or coaches, or an outrageous marketer or someone on YouTube or some pop self-helper with a blog.

These are not philosophers. Philosophy is an understanding

of the fundamental nature of existence. It's a framework for living in this world. There are plenty of philosophers around, but their work rarely makes it into the mainstream.

## AN ENGAGED LIFE

After I started using PeakStorytelling as a framework for organizing how we think about life experiences, ordering them, and then assembling them for performance, people would tell me, "I'd like to reuse this over and over."

And I saw that the method was a philosophy for interpreting life, sorting your blue dots and non-blue dots and where they sit on the hierarchy on the PeakStory map.

It helps you reflect. And reflection leads to an engaged life. And on a large enough level, it becomes a philosophy that enables you to interpret reality as you live it in the way that is most helpful to you.

Religion does that. Self-help groups do that. But they tend to offer a philosophy for *getting through* life. I'm talking about living an *engaged* life.

The PeakStory method has played that role for many people and has become central in how I think about my life. The idea is not to get stuck in the hero place or being only collaborative. You should be living a virtuous life, and you should be looking around at others and imagining that they're at the top of their own PeakStory map, too.

Everyone can live a manifestation of a reflective life that is informed by the pathway, by rolling up from hero to working with others, then discerning what kind of work with others makes us feel truly charged.

The result is that we can emerge as a kind of super-evolved, self-actualized person who can say, "I love this life, and it would be immoral for me to live any other." "I have to teach, I have to be a nurse." "I have to do woodworking and nothing can stop me." "It doesn't matter that I went for engineering, I'm going to be a chef."

And that's the definition of living an engaged life.

By the way, the phrase "an engaged life" might trigger the idea that the unexamined life is not worth living, while the examined life very much is. That notion began with Socrates.

It might be impertinent to take issue with Socrates, but I'm going to say, "Well, maybe…"

## LEVELS OF HAPPINESS

Examining your life isn't enough on its own. You have to integrate whatever you discover in the examination into your PeakStory. You have to move the thing from inside you to the outside, because life is a social sport. Being social is a major source of our happiness. The psychologist and writer Marty Seligman studies happiness and identifies three types: a pleasant life, an engaged life, and a meaningful life.

## PLEASANT LIFE

On the first level, the pleasant life, you're engaged frequently and pretty consistently and doing things that give you pleasure. So in the PeakStory world, this would mean that you're telling your story to yourself and you're batting .500, to use some baseball language. You're flipping the coin heads or tails. Sometimes the story matches what you're doing; sometimes it doesn't.

## ENGAGED LIFE

On the next level, the engaged life, you're living in a way that cultivates, accesses, and grows your strengths, so you're probably batting over .500. You're getting in the zone enough of the time that it's almost habitual. When you think of your story, say, 72 percent of the time, you're thinking of who you are and what you're doing. You're thinking of yourself in a positive way because you're thinking of the positive content of your life making sense en route to where you're going in the next chapter.

## MEANINGFUL LIFE

That's good, but there's one more level: a meaningful life. That's a life marked with purpose, meaning, and real happiness. It comes from what you have learned about yourself from a virtuous standpoint: that it would be immoral for you not to do something that you're motivated to do. At this level, you bring yourself into alignment with the characterization of yourself through the story. In other words, you don't chicken out. This is your story. You lean in and go through, and you say no to things.

A good philosophy should inform the decisions that you make up until the point you make them. And then the decision owns you. If you decide to use the PeakStory method as your life philosophy, your PeakStory will be the pathway to a meaningful life.

Now the only way you can goof it up is to ignore the fact that you're going along this pathway.

## ENACTING YOUR NARRATIVE

To live a meaningful life means you are enacting your narrative all of the time. You're using it to inform yourself as to whether to take this job or that job, whether it's a teaching position or a nonprofit role, or even a promotion that shifts you away from the thing you like to do.

If you love to work with special-needs children, say, and somebody offers you a training job, it might be a chance to enact the PeakStory as a philosophy. The philosophy asks you to go back and look at your narrative and then match it up. What competencies or motivations did you claim? Go back and look at your PeakStory map to see where you are and where you wish to go.

Don't listen to the outside world because you know better.

That's why I say this philosophy goes *beyond* an engaged life. Because a meaningful life is engaged *and* meaningful. And it's more engaged with story matching. It's a click-clack. Does this story click here? Great. Or does it clack? Aw, no.

It's that binary.

You're probably making five to ten decisions about how your story is aligned during the day: which calls to take, which lunch to have with a friend or a former colleague, should you even have that lunch based on your narrative. Don't do things that aren't going to align with the narrative because then you're drifting. Start to clean up your life, and you'll see that this philosophy can add strength to your existence. That's why hundreds or even thousands of people now use the PeakStory model as a philosophy, a guide to living their lives.

They look back at their life and unpack it, which in phenomenology is the way to study the mind through subjective lived experiences. As the famous Renaissance artist Michelangelo said in his eighties, "Ancora imparo—Still I learn."

## NEAR THE PEAK

Your mind is the most powerful processing unit on the planet. Using the right tools is like adding the gearing ratio to an automobile to get the most traction and horsepower converted to the road. When you use the Story Stamp to unpack the past, now, near now, and future possible—connectable chapters of your life—you know that you have stickiness and strength and your story holds up.

That comes from going small to go big.

Think about the decisions you make and how they are leading you to a pleasant life, an engaged life, or a meaningful life. Don't forget it's a hierarchy. A meaningful life is the most rewarding life, because all the research suggests that we all want to have meaning.

Think of the difference between a day you didn't really get up and a day when you properly did, by which I mean days when you got a sniff of a virtuous moment. The day you went to your kid's graduation, or a wedding, or maybe you were doing a project in your yard and a master gardener was going to help you, or you were meeting up with someone to go on a biking journey, or having breakfast with friends you haven't seen in a while. Anything that gives you purpose connects to meaning.

Wouldn't it be wonderful if your life were more like that? That's the difference between using the PeakStory method to get better at self-introduction and using it as a philosophy for living.

The method makes you feel more positive generally because it gives you confidence. It's the confidence you find from trusting your story. Remember, the word "confidence" comes from the Latin *confidere*, meaning to trust fully.

People tend to reciprocate when there is mutuality. You trust your own story, and they will have full trust in you quicker. And it feels good to be trusted. Your story will then move you beyond the storytelling itself to creating meaningful relationships.

## ACCENTUATE THE POSITIVE

The PeakStory method doesn't only show you how to cultivate positive content from your life; it positively encourages you. Even if some of it was negative—and everyone has negative content—you've reframed it. You used it to learn something positive.

This is called a growth mindset, which the Stanford psychology professor Carol Dweck recently made famous in her book

*Mindset.* A growth mindset means that even when something isn't perfect, you can learn something if you frame the negative the right way.

## THE POSITIVITY RATIO

Let me introduce you to the positivity ratio, which has been explored by psychologist Barbara Fredrickson.

Fredrickson figured out the positivity ratio by asking, if you have something negative in your life, how many positive things would you need to reach a net sum zero? Her answer was that the critical positivity ratio is three to one.

In other words, you need three positive events to balance one negative, whatever that negative is. In family affairs, it might be five to one, though maybe that's different in an Italian family or in my Portuguese family, where the ratio might even be seven to one. Hah!

The ratio basically pits flourishing against languishing. Whether you're able to flourish more when you're in a bind is about whether you are around more positivity than negativity.

## KEEP IT POSITIVE

Think about this. If you are a leader in an organization, a group, a family, if you use your story over and over again, are you pumping positivity into your environment? That arena, that room, that conference, that video call? Are you bringing positive language and content into that space? And does that positivity cancel out some of the negativity that may be brought into the collective or because of some random non-positive event?

This is how you start to transform whole places and spaces with your PeakStory, which can help teams or entire organizations.

When several people go through the PeakStorytelling program within a group, whether it's a financial planning group, an audio tech group, a fintech group, I've found that not only do the people telling their stories feel more liberated, but they're also pumping positivity into the group exchange.

People then tend to reference stories a lot of different ways that help insulate against negativity. They now understand that others are capable because they understand each person's contribution. They know their story. How do they know that? Because they understand others' competencies and motivations. Judging happens less, and as teams move toward understanding, they automatically appreciate each other more. They know the grace that comes from the other's hero moment, the collaboration that comes from their working-together moment, and the virtuous moment that matches the role they're in. Cultures are transformed by PeakStorytelling. Isn't that cool?

There's no need for old-school corporate group-think initiatives. Just know your story, know others' stories, and you can change the work story. Story now matters.

This is an inside-outside job. Your story gets spoken to others, and culture change happens. It's a rumble that starts with the individual, then the wave happens when everyone does it, and then everyone gets to ride the wave because everyone's story now matters.

That's super positive.

## GROUP DYNAMICS

Each person finds their three evidence traces in their own PeakStory. Then they hear the same in someone else's story. And another. So the team creates positive traces that they're going to be okay. Collectively, they become armed as a team because they know each other's narratives.

It's like when firms used to send colleagues on team-building retreats. Exchanging stories creates a collective confidence, which then typically creates more adaptability and resilience, which are closely linked. Adapt to survive, but collectively collaborate and thrive as a group, yes?

Stephanie L. Colbry, who was introduced to me by a colleague from Spartan Race, studies groups, and she says they can teach themselves to be dynamically resilient so they can resolve any kind of issue. Well, wouldn't a team be more dynamically resilient because Shannon strengthened Abby, who strengthened Alex? You see the strength that informs their story and their story matches the way they're engaged at work. That way, you start to build up team strength.

## TELLING YOUR STORY

The key to the method is that the story has to be told. It can't remain an internal narrative. It must come out of someone's mouth to spark dialogue, to spark conversation with somebody else. When you can tell your story with different cadence, pace, and pause, and in different venues, at the beginning of speeches, self-introductions, even ad hoc moments, you feel *simpatico*, resonant. You feel like you are where you are with strength and confidence, and people see it and know it. And then you get invited into more conversations.

Congratulations. You've taken the philosophy and enacted it in your life, walking through the world, telling your story in relationship to others and in relation to your own positive-value points.

You'll find that you become more empathetic to others and them to you. Everyone wonders, "Who is John in accounting anyway?" or "Who's the new kid on the block, the transfer in from the competitor's company?" And when you have the courage to tell your story—and it doesn't even require much courage because it's true and because it's not the same sort of put-you-to-sleep story people usually tell—that demystification starts to create relationships.

It moves us beyond the overconnected and underrelated world because now we're relating at work.

### CREATING DIALOGUE

Your story will likely prompt others to respond.

I tend to ask pokey questions to engage another person in my story. I might say, "I used to bike a lot as a kid. Did you bike a lot?" It might be one-to-one, or you might look at a whole audience. You can use this provocatively to open a dialogical exchange, but you have to honor the audience and poke at them and engage them because we live in a world where people want to be engaged.

Dialogue: *dia* means "to pass through your lips," and *logos* means "with meaning." So when you engage in dialogue, you're telling your story and you're making it meaningful in relationship to others.

If you don't engage them, their technology will or their mind will. And they'll escape the moment. Our attention span has fallen over time, which is why it's critical to get your PeakStory right when you get a chance to curate your identity.

When you move from philosophy to performance across audiences but you're consistently stitching with the same sort of material, that gives continuity to your persona. People come to know you. It's like a character in a movie, consistent from scene to scene. We might see different strengths and skills or different characteristics, but they're familiar to us.

### GRINDING GEARS

What if your story clacks more than it clicks? What if everything that makes you feel better, more engaged, and more satisfied suggests you should be in a caring role, but you're a corporate accountant in an intense work environment. You're not getting that satisfaction. The gear of the story doesn't mesh with the gear of workplace.

Well, you could think about switching roles.

But first, how about trying a little alignment, just to check that everything is bolted on the right way? Again, this is the real

Discovery Channel. You're finding out about yourself. You go back to the me-search way of thinking.

Think about your PeakStory. It's both your anchor and your compass. Perhaps you think, okay, I'm an accountant, but I can be a caregiver in this role. Now I use my organizational skills, but in the past, I was a caregiver, so maybe I'm using too many of my analytical skills and not enough of my caring skills. So can I shift my practice, maybe to do some more pro bono work for single moms and dads? Are there other populations I could serve in a pro bono way that would be able to accentuate my caregiving? That way, you don't just lock the doors to your practice. You evolve it to match your story.

Then go back and do a check-in on your PeakStory.

You'll see how you've evolved and written a new part of the future to include a creative way to manifest caregiving without abandoning your current role. You live in the real world, so it may make sense to try it first. You may find you like it a lot, and if you do, you can see there are grants for it, so your next step may be to create a nonprofit. You don't need any more money, so you're just going to build a nonprofit that combines your accounting and caregiving competencies. You're self-authoring now, using your PeakStory to align you.

## REAL-WORLD LIVING

Exactly how you tune your story and mesh your gears depends on the person you are, where you are in your life, and what you need to live. Not everyone is in a position to switch jobs or to work pro bono. We have to earn a buck, right? We live in a world where money is exchanged—but our lives have to align with ourselves, too.

So there's some natural tension there that we should explore.

Misalignment with yourself comes at a cost. Every day, every hour, every minute you're in a grueling "I don't want to be here" situation costs you happiness and fulfillment. You lose the meaning we all crave.

Go back and look at your PeakStory. Where did you make the decision to go here versus there. Can you shuffle through the moment and possibly shift where you are today or could be tomorrow? Can you build something that allows you to get some of the juice you need to get through this so-so space in your life to the other side?

When the timing is right, try making a change. You've done the work, so you're ready, like a fisherman who says, "I've chummed the right spot, so drop your lines. Let's fish." Well, we've chummed, too. Let's story.

The timing of any change will be based on where you are in your life, but don't back out of it. Don't be afraid to tap into your creativity to find a way to move up to living more virtuous moments.

## BE CREATIVE

The psychologist Rollo May called the courage to create "a natural risk." You're going to have to tap into creativity as a response to anxiety at some point in your life's journey.

If your PeakStory isn't fully clicking, apply a little creativity. You have that capacity because creativity is one of the universal competencies, like exploration and leadership. You can build up mental muscles to help you enact parts of your narrative. Look at your competencies. If you have to start influencing people but you see that you haven't been using leadership before, you can figure out a way to do it. If you realize you're low on collaborative moments, you can create more. Don't overthink it. Maybe you don't shove off an opportunity to cook dinner with others before a holiday or share in the grocery shopping responsibilities, because it gives you a chance to exercise that muscle.

Be creative: the answer might not be obvious.

At least now you're aware of what you want and what you can achieve, and how those two things are connected to your storypath. Whatever is the next part you add to your PeakStory will make sense because it will have consistency with what's already there.

It's part of the same story.

## STICK TO THE PLOT

If your plotline is consistent, your themes and threads will make sense of the competencies on which you need to focus. It also allows you to check and say, "Wow, this is the thing I need to tweak." You can see that caregiving is a theme in all your blue dots, yet you're a corporate accountant. How can these two seemingly opposing elements be brought into alignment? Whoever you are, you can bring them together. You see the story first, but there's going to be a sense of feeling it, too. That's the integration part. I once had a client who studied finance, then landed at Columbia for her MBA, but she was also an artist. I'll tell you a bit more later about how she integrated those two parts of her story; but for now, I'll just assure you that she did.

If you need help in leadership, you may want to enroll in a leadership course or certificate program. You don't have to go back and get a degree. There might be a mentor you can approach or a book you can read. What sort of leadership do you need to think about? Communication? Closing sales and generating more business? Relational leadership? What kind of leadership will help you bridge from the now or near now to the future in a way that will accelerate your PeakStory into action?

Don't overcomplicate things. Don't try and force new ingredients into the Story Stamp. Remember the eight competencies:

- Leadership
- Receptivity
- Adaptability
- Discrimination
- Communication
- Organization
- Exploration
- Creativity

Those eight labels are enough. They're fundamental to underlying every one of your behaviors. So as I write this, I'm discriminating as I'm communicating because I'm analyzing language. And I'm doing it with a dash of leadership to make sure that I'm honoring what I know to be true. Or I could go to receptivity and shut the heck up and calm down, and then turn up adaptability if I need to.

We constantly use the eight competencies to orient and reorient ourselves.

They're a discrete set of observations that will help you analyze the choices you make in your life. Use them to ask, "Does my story match how I want to live my life?" You don't just want to answer yes or no. You need to understand *why* it's a yes or no because then you understand how you can shift things if you want to change.

## BRACKETING

Let's say that you have an offer to leave a particular job or go to a particular graduate program, or move to a different town. Go back and look at your blue dots. Zoom in on one. Do you see anything in this blue dot that relates to the decision you have to make?

Just look at the blue dot itself, not your whole story. In phenomenology, we call this bracketing. Bracketing means setting aside emotion and everything else to look at one thing in isolation.

What did you discover? Were there any competencies, any physical space observations, you didn't include in the original description? Maybe it was the time of year; maybe it was an outdoor classroom. Was there anything that happened on the way to the event? Or from the event?

Remember, the moment itself stretches out. Every event in your life begins a little bit before, and it stretches or tapers out a little bit after. That's the way our brain works. We lead up to the event, we have the event, and we lead away from it. That's the way we interpret moments: a lead-up, an event, then an exit.

Like a walk-on and walk-off song.

When you bracket the moment, are you finding in it the power of place? What about the people? Were they interacting with you differently now that you think about it, or was any one person part of the experience more than others? Why might that be true? What competency did that highlight? Were you more of an explorer or more of a contemplator, a wanderer? Did you feel the pressure of a deadline? Did you practice escapism because of that pressure, or did you dig in?

It's all about analyzing what your feeling was *then*.

Go back to the moment. What do you see if you stay with the moment for, say, eight minutes? It feels like a long time, but it's only eight minutes of your life, eleven if you're a real marathoner. When you return to your overarching story, have you discovered anything that gives you more information?

If you do this to every one of your dots, maybe you can add another layer of comprehension and consistency to your Peak-Story. If you do that before a big decision, it will help you see where the decision lies, whether you're moving homes, taking a job, saying yes to a new school, taking a promotion, getting a dog, any sort of decision.

You go back into the capsule of the learning moment. It's almost like a module of learning in your life. The chapter will open up. The more you go back to something, the more you can identify the nuances.

## EXERCISE: CHECK YOUR STORIES

It's time for a checkup.

We've done some big exercises with lots of explanation. This time, you're just going to check your stories.

You're going to match the story you're living to the types of happiness Marty Seligman describes, which is a great way for you to check on your story. The point is to live a life of purpose and meaning where you're contributing and have value.

A pleasant life is when your story isn't engaged fully; it's sort of spotty. An engaged life is when you're engaged most of the time. A meaningful and purposeful life is when the story aligns with what you're really doing with your life, work and nonwork activities nearly all of the time.

Think about dogs or horses. Many have particular purpose: a guard dog or a sheep dog, a barrel-racing horse or an English hunter jumper. How do you see yourself? Are you a horse in the field not being used, so it's kind of pleasant, but you're not really engaged? A pony used to teach new kids? Or a racer using its innate talent, strength, and speed, motivated by the joy of running more than winning the race?

Rank your story, your life. Make a note of what evidence you have for the choice. What can you do to improve it?

Improving your situation is the essence of self-authorship. And by going back and looping, you're matching the PeakStory you created and checking if it is pleasant, engaged, or meaningful right now.

You can look at where your story is claiming to take you and where you are. The delta is the distance you still have to travel to get there.

So how do you close the gap without being reckless? We want to get you to that space where you have stability and purpose, and that feeling gives you a positive charge every morning that you wake up. So if you're a corporate HR person and you want to be working in a high school as a teacher, the first step is to check your engagement level; if it's a little low, remember that your skills could cross over. So you might change jobs. And that might mean that you go to a different community to live, or get rid of your car, or you even share a car. It's sometimes about money, and it's sometimes not about money at all.

It might have to do with more than a change in salary. It might have to do with how you dress, the vacation opportunities you get, whether you see family less or more, whether you have an in-person peer group or whether you have to work remotely. Remember that there's going to be a tension between the amount of money and the amount of meaning when it comes to balancing the two dynamics of maintaining stability and reaching that virtuous next chapter. You are the only one to determine how this process unfolds.

This may not be a life transformation as much as it's transformative to your life.

I'm not judging whatever you want to achieve or wherever you want to go. I am encouraging you to study the three levels of your story to understand their nuances and provide evidence on which to base your decisions for how you live your life.

# CHAPTER 9

## TELLING YOUR STORY

*"Why follow the steps of another to find out where your dreams will lead us?"*

—PETER BLOCK

The PeakStory method is intended to prepare you for high-stakes moments when you need to show your positive value points. But you don't start there. No one dives off the high board before they've practiced a little on the lowest level. Your story is the same. You start low and move up to high-stakes moments.

### LOW STAKES

The first time you tell your story, try it out in a low-stakes situation. Somewhere it's okay if you flub it up. Consider this like a kiddie swimming pool. In other words, you're in the shallow end. No danger of drowning here. It's like trying a football move out in the yard with your nephew. No one really cares if it goes wrong.

Try to get it right, though. You don't want hope to be your

strategy. Low stakes doesn't mean no effort. You still have to work through the method, the structure, and the practice of performing.

Do your prep. You've tried out your story multiple times, recorded it, and listened back. Each time, you've evolved how you nuance each blue dot into the narrative.

Maybe record yourself five times. If the story is only three minutes, it's fifteen minutes total. That's really no time at all.

Listen to yourself. Boy, your story's pretty fascinating. Anyone would want to listen to such an interesting creature now that you've uncovered all this stuff and put it all together.

Now when you go live, you have more confidence. This is full-product self. It's who you truly are, how you see yourself, and how you think others ought to view you. It leaves you and emanates to others because you know your story. If you trust your story, others trust you. It becomes apparent when you share your PeakStory.

Even in low stakes, if someone asked your listeners, "How does this sound?" the answer would be, "He really knows his life," "She really has value here," or "They really know where they're going."

## ONBOARDING YOUR STORY

The chance might come anywhere. It could be in a café, at an airport, on a train. It could be before a formal meeting starts or you and another colleague arrive early for a video call. The other person says, "Hey, what's going on?" And that's an invitation. That's them saying, "So tell me about yourself."

You have to figure out how to onboard your story. You don't say, "I'll tell you a story of my life." Please do not say, "Let me tell you a story." Those things will put people to sleep.

You need a quick on-ramp to the freeway, like, "You know, it's kind of funny. The other day, I was thinking..." and then jump into the story.

To go back to a story I already shared about that US Navy guy turned wealth manager: "It's sorta funny, you know. I'm a wealth advisor. And I never thought that when I was fourteen, having the courage to jump on a train to go from Albany to Manhattan was going to be the start of exploring."

Dot, dot, dot.

Or maybe, "Well, I biked here today, and you know, I've been biking my whole life..."

Dot, dot, dot.

And then you're telling your story.

Don't worry. Be Nike. Just do it, right? And while you're at it, be Apple. Think different, right? Just figure out how some version of your story can go live in a way that isn't the same old story everyone is telling.

## JUDGING YOUR PERFORMANCE

Think about it afterward. How did it go? How did you feel? Did you see their body language, their facial expressions? Were they curious? How was your pace? Did you tell the story quickly? Did you give them an opportunity to play into the conversation?

If I say to my nephew, "Hey, I finally bought another bike," he might say, "I haven't biked in five years." Then you can react to that. It won't be in your PeakStory, but as a human being, you react to what any listener says. And it often provides an on-ramp to your story.

That's the performance: on-ramping your story, telling it, and then off-ramping it.

## MIDDLE STAKES

One takeaway from low-stakes stories is that you're not done. You've begun PeakStorytelling and you're ready to move up to middle stakes. It's an ongoing process because you're look-ing for windows of opportunity to feed your story into the environment, and your story is sounding good. It's bearing more weight.

This is a wonderful time in the process. I got on the phone with someone I was coaching with a background in art, and she said, "I'm using the method to introduce myself to my fellow MBAers, you know? And I see connections to art and finance that I never saw before. I can't wait to share them with my fellow classmates. After all, I'll be spending two years with them. They need to know all of me."

Normally, people would have no idea how art connects with

an MBA program, but my client saw these opportunities to start to tell her story in a mid-stakes situation.

An introduction is not a job interview, true, but this was a Columbia MBA program. You're with those people for two years. And if you flub up the who-you-are story at the start, no one's going to want to work with you. Your cohort won't see your gifts and strengths, or worse, they'll misunderstand you. Or the misslice that you're a quiet finance-oriented person is going to prevail because they don't know about the artist side of you. And by the time they understand who you are at the end of the program, it doesn't have time to impact positively how they relate to you.

## TUNING RELATIONSHIPS

At this stage, you're likely using the method to tune relationships. So when you go from low stakes to mid-stakes, it's usually with other peers, colleagues, people of similar status in an organization. It's not a hiring-firing situation or an "I'm taking over the company" speech. If you're using this book as part of a university program or an initiative within your company, for example, you may have the opportunity to share your story with others in the program.

The benefit is that they start to tune themselves in relationship to you, and you do the same. It's mutual because now you're across from your peer. And I understand who she, he, they are. OK?

There's usually a quid pro quo. People start to unveil more information about themselves. The relationship changes a little because you're so comfortable or because there's commonality or a universality. You're talking about being in the outdoors, camping; you're talking about living by the ocean, or maybe the dog you have that you call Coach, because it helped you when you were feeling isolated as a young man who was a little overweight or whatever. With each deeper exchange, you both move up the PeakStory map toward collaboration and then a virtuous moment.

You have to share information about yourself because when you make yourself a little bit more vulnerable, most people will meet you where you are and be vulnerable in return. That's how relationships start.

## GAINING SUPPORTERS

Now other people know you so that now when you act in a particular way in alignment with your story, living out the philosophy, they're tuned in to the way you want to work, doing the things you want to do, getting the life that you want to live. So what you do doesn't come as a surprise. People who have heard your story are like, "Well, that's the way she is. She always uses creativity and exploration." Or "That guy is such an innovator in technology. He's always problem solving and removing waste from our company, and he's done it since he was a kid. He did it for his uncle's telecommunications company when he was in high school. The guy's crazy smart!"

People who know your story become supporters, which is phenomenal.

## HIGH STAKES

Once you've got some low-stakes and middle-stakes Peak-

Storytelling under your belt, you're ready for the big leagues. You've gotten comfortable with the idea of both the telling and the revealing.

And the more often you do it and the more feedback you get, the more you can tailor it as you move forward.

Every time you tell it in a different environment, remember intention, audience analysis, and context.

- Who is my audience? What skills do they have? Who are they, and where do they sit in the world? What are they likely to be like?
- What is the context of the telling? What place, what time of day? Is it end of day, beginning of the day, the lunch break?
- How am I going to tell this story? Am I excited about it? Should I be a little goofy at the beginning? Like, "Every time I look in the sky, I think of this pilot friend of mine, whom I went to Rochester with, where I showed up like a science geek…"

In other words, how am I going to get to this story about being a science geek in this situation? Well, I've got a map I'm going to use, so first I need to figure out how to get there.

A lot of times, it could be as easy as this: "So just the other day, I was thinking about when I was an undergraduate at the University of Rochester and how I was such a science geek, a far cry from the cool BMX kid that I used to be back home. It was weird because I was a BMXer and used to race all over New England. Looking back, I can see that this brings me right to being quite an innovative professor, though, trying to map out different ways to use rhetoric. My exploration and pioneering nature was alive when I was a racer and is also alive now as a professor. I just add a little bit more creativity now, and I'm not competing for a win for myself; I'm helping others get the win by winning audiences over. That means I help people express their identity to people who might otherwise, quite frankly, make shit up about them or not see them for their full value and worth."

Okay. Then the person listening starts to know me so they can be a bit more honest in return. Be sure you know what talent you want to turn up in a storytelling episode so the listeners will become truly tuned to you. And you can do this before you start to speak because you know the sort of person they are and the version of your PeakStory they would prefer.

## SOCIAL CUES

Look out for social cues. Because you've done the PeakStory method, you don't have to focus on raking through what lived experience to share. You know your story. So you're just bending it by being alert to social cues. You stick to the integrity to your story. You're not revamping it, you're not running away from part of it, you're not making it up. You're just tuning it to the audience.

You're being a good teacher. A good listener.

You bring up your Australian shepherds, and it turns out the listener is allergic to dogs and cats. So what do you do now?

If you do what most people do, you mention that someone in your life has allergies, too. This is not a useful response.

Instead, stay in your story. Of course, you could say, well, I don't really like my dogs, but that would be weird because you have three of them. So you cut it short. You don't deny what's important to you, but maybe you say, "Well, one of the reasons why I like my dogs is they're really smart. And when people come around my home and they're not able to be around dogs because of an allergy or something, I can just say, 'Crate.' The dogs go upstairs to their crate. You don't even know I have a dog in the house. You should let your friends know if they want to protect you from this allergy, they need a smart dog, whatever kind it is."

So you stand in your story, but then your creativity and adaptability come into play because you're open. You're hearing all of the cues, and you have already discerned your story.

You are the teacher of your story. A teacher's job is to engage the audience, and the capacity to do that comes from creativity and the adaptability of a story within what I call the situated telling. The storytelling is situated or seated in a particular moment, in a particular context.

## STAY OPEN

Pretend you have an openness dial, and turn it up to ten so that you be fully tuned in to the people, the place, and the vibe. Be aware of the environment in which you're telling the story, which means look at facial expressions, the eye contact, any furrowed brows or looks of confusion. Look at the room. Now scan the area. Are there artifacts that say, this person's an achiever producer or they overly celebrate great accomplishment? Or are the folks proud of being rewarded here, or do you see signs of being caregivers or philanthropists, or of being socially humanitarian in supporting causes? Explore business profiles and read social media postings so that you're doing honor to the people you're with and telling the story that they're more likely to be tuned in to.

The more open you are, the more you can analyze and synthesize details. When you do so, it sparks a dialogical exchange. That makes you feel more personally connected to your listener, and the storytelling episode instantly unfolds in a paced and pleasant way for them. It becomes an encounter and not a transaction.

They start to talk a little bit more, which creates relational empathy that leads into heightened cultural consciousness and contextual awareness. In other words, now you know more about the culture of this workplace or they understand the context of the work that you do or the thing that you're trying to team up on for a project. You're more tuned in to each other. That's cool. Better still, that's the point. You'll feel it.

Even though you're telling your story to claim value, you also end up learning more about others. That allows you to tweak and tune your unfolding and walk away with valuable information so that you can honor this relationship with a bit of ease and grace. It might also create quicker trust formation and assimilation into the work you're about to do in a school project or corporate setting or whatever.

Be open to information, to the environment, then synthesize your story to fit. Be prepared for dialogue and pause. Be prepared to feel more connected to who you really are and understand that that's an attractive feature of PeakStorytelling.

And understand that you're going to know more about the other person as an outcome because it's so natural.

## TUNING THE STORY

The more you think this way, the more natural it becomes. Also, the more reps you do with your story, the more willing you are to adapt on the fly to new information that hits your windshield. You can start a story one way, then the listener reveals something about themselves or something happens at the dinner table while telling your story. And now you can adapt, slow play, or pick up the pace despite an interruption because you know one dot, two dot, three dots. You own the story now.

Let's go back to our US Navy guy and wealth manager. He's about to talk to a prospect who's a former marine, and he's not aware of that. The prospect says, "I don't like a lot of chitchat and small talk when it comes to my investments."

Well, in that case, our guy might flatten the dot. Or maybe add a little bravado to it. It's just like what you do in writing. Think about a letter writing exercise in school, where you had to write to the principal, the president, a senator, a government official. You write each letter differently because each has a different audience. It's key to know what areas to flatten or embellish. This is the essence of tuning your story.

So if you find yourself talking to a marine, or a military person, or an engineer, you know that those people are more analytical. They tend to use less language than people who are artistic. They don't like people to talk a lot. So don't overcommunicate. So our guy just says, "Look, I'm a safety officer at heart. I like to analyze things. Measuring risk started on a train trip with my dad. At least, that's how my informal training happened." So now the marine does the doggy head tilt, and our guy gets the chance to onboard his fuller story because he overcame the initial barriers by watching and listening to the marine and fed pieces of his story in carefully and cleverly to create interest. So the marine says, "I like you."

If you then learn that when the marine retired, he became a yoga instructor, you adjust again to appeal to his flexible nature.


## A CAUTIONARY TALE

It's important to remember with the PeakStorytelling method not to run before you can walk. Things can go wrong.

I've got a friend, Peter, whose family ran a 150-plus-year-old manufacturing company. He's addicted to storytelling. We were talking one day about Maslow's hierarchy and he said, "You know, Dr. D., I think it's all flipped. Everybody's looking to do what they want to do at the top of the triangle but without doing the stuff underneath."

It's the same with the PeakStory map. Don't leave out your hero or your collaborator story and just tell your virtuous story. That's like the people Peter complains about because they say, "Hey, I really want to be able to write this book or run this company," but they have no evidence to support their claim. There's no foundation. The parts of the triangle are missing that show me that you can overcome obstacles or work with others in a fashion that would make me believe that you have the value and worth to be credentialized as the next leader or team member or whatever.

Don't skip the base or the middle. Stay tuned in to your story, and don't remove the data just because you're excited about the peak. Because the listener needs that information to be able to substantiate where you're headed as you spiral up. This is critical.

It can be the other way, too. People sometimes overtell their hero story. It runs away with them. Check yourself. Check how much of the story you're unpacking. Like a soccer player or a basketball player, don't dribble on the spot over and over. At some point, you need to move forward in your story. So don't overly ground it in one place.

Look at how much you're unpacking one part of your story over the others. So always check yourself.

## PUNCHED OUT

I have a student who is an executive leader who works in public relations. He helps Christian leaders in retreat settings. He called one day, and I asked how he was doing. And he said, "Everything's good, Doc. I got punched in the nose." I said, "You got punched?" He said, "Yes. Well, actually, it wasn't the nose. I got hit very hard in the sternum."

He was with some football players and wrestlers and was talking to them about their testimony as being men of God. One of these guys was sharing about a relationship, so my guy tells him, "You've gotta straighten this out because it's going to affect the way you mentor other followers."

This gargantuan human being, a former wrestler, got involved in the conversation and said, "Who gives you the right to start talking like that? Who are you to be giving out advice to us?"

"What do you mean? Who am I?" My guy rose and matched this guy's machismo energy. He became strong.

My guy is a PR guy who is typically so well mannered, but he was running hot. "Who am I? I'm the one who just received an email from this guy…" He showed him an email from a VIP in the media.

So then the wrestler shrugs as if to say, "Who's this guy telling anybody how they should be talking about relationships?"

My guy flipped. He left his story in his back pocket. He came off track. Holding up the mobile phone was the wrong move. The right move was to hold up his story.

So then the wrestler hit him.

I asked my guy, "What were you thinking?"

"I wasn't thinking, Doc. He got to me."

You have to be receptive when you tell your story in the world. When you feel your emotions rise, don't get derailed. Exhale and fall into your story. It'll save you, even during times of conflict.

It could help you dodge the punch.

## AN UNTOLD STORY

Right off the bat, my guy should have used his story. Part of his story is that he was a little overweight when he was younger, so he should have started there. So the other guy would say, "What do you mean?"

I put myself in my guy's shoes. "'Yeah. I was an overweight kid who didn't have a lot of friends, and my dog's name was Coach. And you want to know why his name was Coach?' The guy's going to go, 'What do you mean? Why?' 'Because he coached me through feeling pretty depressed, kind of fat and not in shape. Walking this dog helped me process through a lot of things. I'd talk to him while we walked, and it allowed me to feel comfortable joining inner-city teams, where I was the only white kid playing basketball and that helped me lose weight and work with people from diverse backgrounds. I felt included. They felt included, even though I was very, very different from them. So I find that profiting through adversity is really critical.

'And being a good listener is a really critical skill to have. And in the spirit of serving everyone as a media director here, my role is simply to try to create connection and to make sure everybody feels okay, just like that dog.'"

That's what I told him. My guy exhaled, smiled, and said, "Aw, Doc, that's it."

I said, "All I did was take your story parts and play with them. Your hero story was not feeling accepted and feeling a little depressed with Coach the dog. Your collaborative moment was playing basketball. Your virtuous moment is being a man of God who uses a Christian leadership style and helps articulate other people's media messages. That's your PeakStory. And then you got stuck because someone derailed you."

Well, at some point, anyone could be derailed when telling their story. Don't worry about it. You can be imperfect. Don't worry about it.

Just don't get punched in the chest like my guy. Don't pick fights with people twice your size.

## ADJUSTING THE PROCESS

If you've done the reps in the low and mid-stakes, you're more acutely aware in high stakes of what's happening, and your PeakStory becomes second nature. It is who you are.

Remember, there's no suggestion that you're done. You're walking through life, collecting new dots and interpreting them, but now you have a guide. There will be some adjustments to be made along the way, which you can resolve by continuing to use the tool. Over time, your core dots may shift and adjust or be replaced by new dots. It only makes sense that dots may change and have different priority over time as the process of living never stops.

Your core story remains the same, but consider how you transform and use it as a relational tool to influence how people think of you in a positive way. That is how you keep it at the heart of how you live and how you use it as a performance tool to deeply represent who you are and who you are becoming.

## STORY SPOTTING

Now that you've taken time to study who you really are, it's like you have a PhD in yourself. Congratulations. It's a rare thing to know yourself as well as you possibly can.

How about others? How well do you know them? Can you spot the formative experiences in their stories?

Learning by observing others comes naturally to us as human beings. When I learned Brazilian Jiu-Jitsu, my instructors would always say, "Hey, can you see what he's doing?" Sometimes I hear my daughter Abby learning how to quilt with her grandmother, Sandy. I hear the sewing machine going a few rooms away, and Sandy says, "Do you see how we flip the fabric?" and Abby goes, "Oh, yeah, right." Her grandmother always invites her to look at something. "What did you see there?"

Good managers and teachers give students an opportunity to spot applied learning because that's when students can show what they've internalized from a learning process. Surgeons in training follow the learning sequence of watching a procedure the first time, performing it the second, and teaching it the third.

I *know* y'all have been a good student.

You know that the hero story is about you overcoming an obstacle for yourself. You know that collaboration is about not just belonging; it's also about working with others to *create* something. And the virtuous moment comes when you think, "I love this thing" and you lost track of time.

So now that you can recognize these stories, you can start to spot them all around you.

## LEARN FROM OTHERS

The PeakStory method is a frame of reference for interpreting other stories than your own. So let's go spot some stories.

Where can you find them? Well, you could listen to TED

Talks if you prefer to spot stories from the comfort of your own home or office. Listen to how speakers introduce themselves, state their credentials. Or you could read a book. Or maybe you're taking a bike ride and you want to listen to some stories, so you take an audiobook or call up a podcast or two.

Maybe it's something like David Goggins's book *You Can't Hurt Me*. It's a story by a former US Navy SEAL about physical and mental achievement. I listened to it while I was walking my dog. I thought about his story, so instead of walking, I took the dog for a quick run. I asked myself, "What's the worst that's going to happen anyway?"

That's how Goggins overcame obstacles. He was always overcoming them by himself, and his collaboration really didn't happen in the most formative way until he was in the SEALs. Goggins went on to do ultramarathons such as Badwater. Once when he landed in Nevada where he was supposed to walk part of a marathon, he ended up running the whole thing and qualified for the Boston marathon, which he ran in three hours and eight minutes.

Goggins is a great example of someone with obstacle immunity. He searches them out and obliterates them. If you want an example, grab his book. But beware: there's a little cussing once in a while! If you don't like cussing, you could read *Finding Ultra* by my friend Rich Roll. It's another book about running.

Whichever book you choose, try to find some collaborative stories that might have been formative for either guy. Can you see where each guy's virtuous story starts to emerge? Give it a go!

If you don't want to learn about ultramarathoners or athletes, try reading about Michelle Obama or Jerry Seinfeld even. In his show *Comedians in Cars Getting Coffee*, Seinfeld interviews other comedians about their life stories. It's another great source to learn from others.

## PICK YOUR MATERIAL

You can do this with any book that is autobiographical or reliant on lived experiences. TED Talks are full of moments erupting to the top. They're not PeakStories, which are deeper, but in most talks, you'll see moments that rise. You might be able to see a connection to why a person did the TED Talk and their story path, or you might not see it at all, depending on the style of the talk.

Go back and read or listen to Steven Jobs's 2005 Stanford speech, or sit in a café and tune in to conversations. Try being a professional eavesdropper.

(Obviously, don't just become a conversation snooper for the sake of it!)

You'll hear stories that you recognize. Maybe a story has the essence of a hero or collaborative story, even if you're not spotting perfectly aligned blue dots. It might not happen every time. Think of it like stargazing when the night is sometimes clear but sometimes cloudy. You might have to be really thoughtful and focused to find the essences.

Watch how people respond. When they hear a hero story, do they look like, "Wow, that person's tough or strong or can accomplish things"? Notice the speaker, too. Are they energized when they tell a story? Do they shift tone? Does their voice sound more engaging? Are they more engaged?

When you hear people talk, it's fascinating how they return to the past, but at the same time, they're hopeful about the future. There's rarely any methodology for bringing the two together.

## OTHER PEOPLE'S DOTS

When you get good at spotting stories, you hear a lot of versions of dots, a lot of types of story paths. But you might also notice that, wow, people don't really connect the dots. You hear that they're excited about a dot, but they don't connect it; they don't move to the next tier of the PeakStory.

Worse, they add their own interpretive nonsense.

Most times, there's nothing you can do. It's not *your* dot, dammit. It's the other person's dot. All you can do is listen and try to lay up moments of connection, try to harvest some good stuff, because you're completing their narrative in your head—that's the risk when you don't connect your dots.

It's frustrating, but you don't get to tell anyone else's story. Stick to your own. But that's not to stop you listening to how a college kid is announcing his plans to go to law school, having an uncle who is already a lawyer, and figuring that there is some genetic connection with his uncle's ability to analyze, advocate, and communicate as an attorney. Against popular belief, being an attorney doesn't just run in the family.

*Guiding Advice*

Also, where you see someone put on the spot to introduce themselves—remember, "Tell me about yourself"—maybe you can spot what their stories *should be*. They speak with absolutely no idea where they're going, no clue of the information they want to give you. They can't put it together in a way that makes sense, but perhaps you can. Or perhaps there simply is no story.

It might be possible, if it's a peer or someone on your team or who trusts you, to call a timeout and say, "Hey, you know, you need to think about how you're presenting your story." Or maybe it's not for someone in your position to do if they're in a more senior position than you. Don't worry. Senior folks do a good job looking after themselves. But in the world of the flip, everyone needs some feedback and another chance to tell their story.

So perhaps you hear someone introduce themselves, maybe a new member of the team. And they flub it up. You can say, "Let me tell you something I think might be helpful to you professionally." Explain that if they learn to storypath, people will feel more at home with who they are at work.

If this book's been helpful to you, tell them. You could even give them a copy. Or tell them to contact Dr. D. Ha!

## ENGAGING AT WORK

As I discussed at the beginning of the book, the way people introduce themselves pretty much all sounds the same. It's difficult to listen to the same humdrum or put-me-to-sleep stories. So what are we doing to fix this? In organizations, we need to come to know our people quicker so that they know one another quicker, so that they engage and collaborate faster so that the organization is more productive.

Productivity is all about aligning skills with job competencies. If you have this particular competency, you will fit best in this place in the organization. But if I don't know more about you, or your employer doesn't know more about you, they might not find this out for three and a half years. Maybe longer. Maybe never. You continue to be an accountant with a caregiver's heart, when maybe you're better suited to human resources.

Years ago—and it still holds true—a Gallup poll suggested that two-thirds of the US payroll is being wasted because people are actively disengaged at work. Two-thirds. Think about it. People pretend to work, they talk about work, but they're not actually working.

And neither the employers nor the employees know what to do about it.

## GOING OFF TRACK

People start getting off track early. They begin to suspect they're off track when they're younger, but they never get any guidance or they get the wrong guidance. "Study engineering; you'll never be without a job," a well-meaning grandparent who grew up in the Depression says, even though you think being a songwriter would be cool, you tuck that dream away. They don't learn in middle school how to make decisions that will become a healthy manifestation of what will be, after four years, the ultimate college essay of what they want to do in their life, what vocation they have chosen. Then they're off to college, and they explore and some get interested and engaged, but others disengage and take a long time to complete college. They're working longer, but they 're working less—and bear in mind that this is the generation that is most motivated to do meaningful work in areas such as social causes.

Storypathing helps them process that. It engages them to be reflective and connects their interests to work and their own lived experiences. That's a powerful triad.

But if we don't get a methodology in place to achieve that, whether it's through HR, through student success centers, or through high school guidance, we'll be on track for having more than two-thirds of the payroll wasted, maybe seven or eight people out of ten eventually.

We're teaching people how to be imposters at work versus being themselves, and it's not good for ourselves, let alone society. We need to unleash personal identity at work to maximize engagement and happiness. Then that will pour over from work to personal life, and recreational life, and spiritual life and into our communities. Then people feel more integrated and more engaged.

The PeakStory method is a way of engaging with life. So you're more aware, you're more vigilant. You are more able to story spot. You can see the blue dots at the base of stories, whether they belong to you or someone else. So let's look at how you can keep storypathing at the heart of your life.

## EXERCISE: TURNING STORY PRO

It's fun to spot other people's stories.

We did it with the Steve Jobs's commencement speech.

You can literally sit beneath a tree and watch TED Talks, speeches, and autobiographies on your favorite handheld device, or if that's not your cup of tea, you can read work essays and cover letters.

Try spotting the dots within the story. Tag the moments. Do you see a hero dot, a collaborative dot? Or did a guy skip from hero to virtuous, and totally leap over collaborative, so you have no evidence the dude can even work with others.

You'll see gaps in people's stories. You'll find other examples where you're attracted to the story and you'll be able to see why.

Keep notes in your journal. Where did you hear or read the story? What were the dots? What worked and what failed? How can you apply anything you've learned to your own story?

You're starting to turn pro. You're going from an amateur story-teller to a pro because you're spotting the constituents of another pro. It's like a taste test for a chef.

Speechwriters do it all the time. They spot other people's speeches and look for the parts that make it compelling. And you've become a speechwriter for your own life.

Check the stories. See if you can find hero, collaborative, and virtuous within the same performance.

Remember, the more you spot dots in other people's stories, the more that awareness will help tune your story and how you tell it.

You'll also see where people are effective and not as effective.

Your internal drive to share your story will grow, and you'll become more analytical of your lived experiences. You're anticipating how to unfold your story with speed and use less energy on recalling the parts and more energy liaising it or sharing it in different environments.

# CHAPTER 10

———

# THE ULTIMATE CONNECTOR

*"How do you change the world? One room at a time. Which room? The one you are in."*

—PETER BLOCK

I've already quoted Edmund Husserl, "I must achieve internal consistency." And Kierkegaard, who said that "life can only be understood backwards; but it must be lived forwards."

Husserl and Kierkegaard remind us that everything connects: our dots, our stories, other people's stories, the world around us. I call the PeakStorytelling method the ultimate connector because it makes you a participant, not a spectator.

Let's not forget, we're all overconnected and underrelated. In a world of mobile devices and apps that link us to profiles, avatars, a universe of data, we mistake empty connections for real relationships. We lose track of the stuff that really matters.

Remember we talked about provisional identity claims on social media and how they often crumble when they come into contact with reality?

Some people suggest technological innovation will help us be more engaged. In theory, it will let us free ourselves from repetitive, unrewarding tasks—whether it's office work or true assembly-line work—so we can get on with a higher order of activities: being creative, thinking, engaging.

Yeah, right.

That's not what actually happens. Instead, technology creates distractions that form habits, and everyone gets pulled into a vicious snowball effect that rolls up our free time in an avalanche of digital digressions.

Think of your life right now. How often do you feel you need a deliberate unplug? A technology break? A long walk in nature or a work out? These disconnections give us space, like meditation, because they take us back to the kind of lives we had as kids: real connections, real relationships.

## A PRIMAL FORM

Story is a way of returning to a primal way of being in order to stabilize oneself. Storypathing offers a way back to real relationships because your story muscle is your relationship muscle, too.

You might have lost the muscles over time. Life's busy. It's not really your fault, but it doesn't matter. Storypathing will let you reclaim those mental muscles. But—and I can't say this often enough—those muscles can still waste away if we don't continue to use them. (That's why I call them muscles because they can get stronger *or* weaker depending on how you use them.)

## LIFETIME TRAINING

You've exercised to build your PeakStory. You've told it in low-, mid-, and high-stakes situations. You've strengthened your mental muscles. You know the obstacles that you've overcome to create hero stories, how you've worked with others in collaborative stories, the virtuous stories of the things you love to do, that it would be immoral for you not to do.

Now you have to keep telling your story. Repetition is key. You don't have to tell your story like an automaton. No artificial intelligence here! You do the drills so you can repeat the core parts in different orders in different contexts in different ways.

That's your lifetime training program.

You use the highlighted two, three, or even four competencies that have fueled you over time to give you consistency and to animate your story. They create a real, animated version of you, not an abstract. You make known your motivations.

Once that happens, you're more likely relating to other people, not just showing up for a brief connection. You gain more relational power, whether you're doing the process as part of leading a team, to build a business, or to sell something, whether you're the new leader in your organization or a new teacher, whether you're running a professional development workshop or you're doing an internship—anywhere someone might say, "Tell me about yourself."

## BETTER YOUR GAME

You don't see NBA basketball players skipping warm-ups. They still line up to do layouts and jump shots before all games. Do you think the pros miss a chance to take some shots?

Of course not.

They always move toward opportunities to better their game. It's the same for you and your PeakStory. To better yourself, it's all about moving toward those chances to unpack your story, to feed it into new places and spaces.

To join the ranks of the pros, repetition is critical. It's all about increasing your reps. Repetition creates success. Comedian Jerry Seinfeld is notorious for note-taking on a yellow legal pad as he reworks his own jokes over and over, right up to the moment before he steps up to the mic. NFL players in pre-season or actors preparing for a take are the same. Again and again. Repetition and variance are muscle builders behind any performance. Keep examining your performance. Where do you think you are in terms of your content? Are the connections clear? Are there areas where you have to have a bit more credentializing? How does your personal style affect the ways you can stretch your story to be able to get this identity claim out there in a particular storytelling moment?

The work doesn't finish. But there is good news.

You're not making up this story. All these things really did happen to you. You're just conveying the story in a particular way.

## SPIRALING UP

The PeakStory method is so flexible that it will remain relevant as you move through life, no matter when you begin—but only if you keep using it.

You might be tempted to say, "Hey, I've read the book. I'm ready for the speech, the interview, the high-stakes networking event, whatever it is." Or "I got through some trouble in my life, and I feel a sense of internal cohesion. I feel a little bit more like pulled together by this. Wow! It's better than the therapist."

Take it from me, that's not what you should say.

You're right that you've gotten through this, you've created your story, you can check the box—but you can't stop now.

We all want to check off milestones. It's how we track our own development. At thirteen, you figure out something about your childhood days. Tick. Or at eighteen, you *really* figure out your high school days as you're about to go to college. Tick. And then you have your pre-midlife crisis, your midlife crisis, your career switch. Tick, tick, tick.

Any milestone, any switch, works better when it's mindful rather than mindless, because everyone is spiraling up or hoping to spiral up to a stage where we can do work that matters to us. So whenever you move from something you do a lot to something else, use your story muscle. It'll help you figure out where you need to go to next.

## WIRED FOR STORY

I want to share one of my favorite phrases: A lived life has a lot of content.

It seems obvious. But how often do you stop and consider how much stuff you've done, seen, felt?

That's a lot of possible content for any single PeakStory. But that means there's even more benefit in being able to tell it your way. It not only creates the version of you that shows your true value and worth. It also changes you neurologically. Your brain rewires because of your newfound story.

According to neuroscientist David Eagleman, all the neurons in the brain are fighting for attention, and the brain reconfigures itself accordingly. He uses the phrase "chronic adjustment" to describe how the brain adapts to anything new: to learning, to adversity, to telling your story. That means the brain is not destined to story in just one way. It can chronically adjust itself, realign its neural pathways, to sculpt itself to your story and your talents.

As you configure and tell your story, your brain adjusts. So you're no longer the same person as when you set out. In fact, you've already changed since you started reading about the PeakStorytelling method because you have gone back to recount the experiences in your life. You have learned what meaning and purpose look like, given your current role or about-to-get role, the thing you're about to do or the job you're about to have. Not only do you feel different about where you are, but you *are* different because your brain processing is different.

### The Changing Brain

Eagleman describes *neuroplasticity*: the ability of your brain to change neural pathways. If you feel uncomfortable about your story but you're confident in the confines of your office, your room, or you have tight friendships that you feel at ease, here's the good news. As your story changes, your brain changes and you'll eventually feel more confident in sharing your PeakStory. Be patient. As the title of Eagleman's book puts it, you're "livewired." What does that mean? It means you're in charge. You are the software driving the way you develop and become—including the hardware of your brain itself. You are in control as to how you move through life. You are the ultimate self-author.

Eagleman explains the difference between an amateur soccer player and a professional. An amateur often gets the ball stolen. You've seen this in pickup games, maybe experienced it yourself. You know what I mean.

That doesn't happen to the pro.

Why not? In terms of neuroscience, the amateur player is conscious of all of his or her movements. They typically signal what they're about to do on the pitch: their body language, their facial expression, their movement. So the ball gets stolen. The pro, on the other hand, is livewired to act without thought, so there's no signal of what they're going to do. Any signal they give off is probably a trick designed to get the tackler to bite so the pro can move on with the ball. They don't lose their place or their progression downfield.

How does this relate to storytelling? Well, when you start out telling your PeakStory—when you're still an amateur—you're going to be aware of all the different dynamics: the people in the room, the stakes, what you look like, what you're wearing. You know you can't let the ball get stolen away because that ball is your story, so you do lots of pre-prep and tell your story in low-stakes or mid-stakes environments before you try high stakes.

When you become a story "professional," two things happen. Number one, the speed at which you adjust your story gets quicker so you can land it in a particular setting, relationally, to somebody who is new to you or somebody who just walks in the room. In other words, your speed to story improves.

Number two, it's going to take much less effort. Of Eagleman's two soccer players, the amateur uses more brain activity, not the pro. Surprised? You shouldn't be. The amateur is hyper-vigilant to his or her actions, whereas the pro is one with the game, relaxed and confident. When you are one with your story, it's far easier to move in and out, changing your performance of it.

Your PeakStory is reshaping you, neurologically. And every time you storypath, you become more conscious of the different nuances. The better you become at being one with story, the more you become livewired for storypathing your life.

You're equipped to move forward. Confident, right? (Remember the Latin, *confidere*, to trust fully.) And mindful that you're going to pick up nonverbal cues and tone of voice and you're going to shift and shrink parts of stories at different times.

What's changed? You've created a meta-awareness of yourself, which helps you live a meaningful life.

## CLAIMING OPPORTUNITIES

If you stick to your story, it provides a way in to relationships. You become the ultimate connector. You can use your story to get yourself heard within the virtuous realm of the work that you want to do.

Remember we talked about the flip?

The flip is real. Anyone can tell their story, from leader to follower, because today everyone has the same storytelling privileges. Workers have almost as much power as the people with formal power.

The key is, you have to *Story Like You Mean It*.

Are you claiming those windows of opportunity for storytelling?

Because that's how the PeakStorytelling method will get you to that virtuous chapter. It provides advocacy for the thing you're claiming that you want and deserve. It shows how your skills have strung together this theme for your life. It transports the listener back in time, then to the future, so they can know that you're okay. Whether you're a wealth advisor, a teacher, an artist, a community developer, a caregiver, a medical doctor, a military person, a first responder, the story of how you got there is the most compelling validation of why you occupy that place today.

If you're missing out on telling your story, you're not seeding people's brains. You're not planting the idea of yourself. The more you seed, the more people invite you to the party. The more people start to tell your story, the more your story becomes resellable. People become interested in you. You're now worth remembering.

Hesitation isn't your friend. You need to be ready to go, wired for story.

As we've seen, the modern worker wants self-expression and meaning making. PeakStorytelling is a method to achieve it. It's a model to build it, tell it, repeat it, evolve it, get power from it, use it, or teach it.

## FIND YOUR STORIES

PeakStories are all around us. People are constantly reaching out, attempting to make connections. There are lots of examples, depending on who inspires you. We've explored Steve Jobs and his famous commencement speech, and I referenced the David Goggins book. The mayor of Atlanta, Keisha Lance Bottoms, has told her story. You're tuned to hear these stories now.

Take Joe De Sena, the founder and CEO of Spartan obstacle-course racing, who recently bought out a competitor, Tough Mudder. People like Joe who are telling their full story and can connect it to enterprise, especially when they're entrepreneurial or leading an initiative, create so much resonance in the world. Aren't you curious why this former Wall Street guy, Joe D., started an obstacle-course racing company, which is now the largest obstacle-racing company in the world?

Look at a musical artist such as Maggie Rogers, who was discovered in a masterclass at NYU being taught by Pharrell Williams and whose unique type of folk dance got her a nomination for a Grammy.

Why did Maggie's music career take off, or Joe's business, or the self-help career of David Goggins? It's because what they do is linked to their identity.

Whatever your mission, it's based on your identity. When you hear these stories, you understand people; you get why they're good at what they do.

### Identity Claim

I have a friend named Jimmie Allen from Delaware. Jimmie's a black country-and-western singer, and there aren't a lot of them. Darius Rucker, maybe Aaron Neville, Cowboy Troy, and of course, Charley Pride.

I met Jimmie, and his story had a lot of hero elements to it. I was president of Alex and Ani Corporate University, building up their learning institute and advising executives on their stories. I remember getting him on stage at the Peace Love Charity event, and at the time, he had already earned some praise from *American Idol* appearance. Today, he is one of the top new artists in country music. His breakout single, "Best Shot," was a big hit.

But Jimmie used to sleep in cars and had to use his gym membership to take a shower. Then he collaborated with Alex and Ani and would play in their retail jewelry stores before he eventually moved to Tennessee and really found his genre, which was country rather than pop.

Everything came together for him and his story. My daughter couldn't believe I knew him. I told her, "Nobody starts because it's easy. You know, this guy slept in cars." She's like, "Are you kidding me? Have you seen his Ford pickup truck? It's so unique. It's amazing, Dad!" I said, "So is he."

Jimmie has a great truck. He's collaborating with Darius Rucker. And he's got a lot of good things going.

Jimmie's a phenomenal human being, but he became awesome because he defied the odds to follow the path, and the story he's written for his own life honors the dots he collected along the way and fits the identity he has today to a T.

## LIVEWIRED TO STORY

Jimmie Allen's tale is a great example of what happens when someone becomes livewired to story.

You know that because that's what's happened to you. You've become livewired to story. You've chosen the moments in your story because you know that when they're put together, they convey your value and worth in the work you do, the life you lead, or the change that you are searching to make in whatever part of your life.

You have a call to story. It reminds me of a manifesto I created many years ago to use in my TEDxPublicStreet talk. I called it *Story Like You Mean It*.

That was the time I found out what my story needed to be/come. Now that the power of story is real in your life, may the manifesto help you claim your next chapter.

*Story Like You Mean It!*

This is your STORY.

Story like you mean it.

If you aren't in character, JUMP IN.

You've been divinely placed here for a reason.

Honor your calling & act on it with purpose.

LOVE is within all of us; show us yours.

Your work is YOUR (+) STORY.

Give back as a practice. Interconnect.

To story is human.

Consciously create a collaborative one.

Judge less. Invite more. Be at peace.

You are BLESSED. Retell the POWER of story with LOVE. STORY your DREAM. Settle your soul.

INSPIRE by DOING.

© Dennis Rebelo

## EXERCISE: LIVING WITH STORY

Think back to the start of the book when you started listening for other people's stories. Think of all the stories you heard, the zone-outs and the standouts.

Now it's your turn. Game time.

You have the right to tell your own story. You have the plan and the process.

You're wired for story.

The key to preserving your story is to keep it fresh, and that means you have to use it. Be on the lookout for opportunities where the application can be immediate because storytelling is a muscle that needs to be exercised.

Now that you've got the workout plan and you're wired for story to show your value and worth, you can light up rooms, places, and spaces with your narrative. So is it going to be here? Is it going to be there? Or there? Or there? You have to know when to turn the lights on. When to light up a room and light up space with your narrative to show that you have value in work.

When are you going to feed this story into the environment as the ultimate connector or relater?

Look at your coming week, look at your month, look for chances. Now that you live through your story, you can now roll in and highlight the value that you're likely to give to a team.

There are many ethics to storytelling. Follow the basics: Don't lie. Don't use your story to deceive or cheat. Respect yourself and others.

You will not zone out again if you use your PeakStory. You will not sleepwalk into rooms or meetings. You will not go into conference rooms, interviews, sales events the same way ever again. And you will see shifts in the way people react to you. And those shifts are real because you've altered your brain and perhaps their brain, too, in the process. You've done it all yourself, this social and neurological shifting that you've been able to accomplish. Wow!

You've reclaimed self-authorship, and you've probably activated even more competencies. Because now you've reclaimed the power of story.

---

# CONCLUSION

## STORY LIKE YOU MEAN IT

At the beginning of this book, we set out to teach you a method to create a story that represents you but also to claim an identity that fits where you are right now, en route to the work or life that you want.

If you think the PeakStorytelling method is all about saying who you are and gaining a value, or replacing a misslice, well, yes, it is. And it's also about engaging in general conversation in a world where that has become rare. It helps us forget about technology and replaces it with the best gift in the world: presence.

You know the elements by now: hero, collaborative, and virtuous. They make sense because everybody, no matter what they do, from a trades person to a surgeon, everybody has had a hero moment where they have overcome an obstacle. Everyone has tried to work together, whether it was successful or not. And everyone is doing something they love or wishing to do something they love, which is virtuous.

When you combine these parts in your story, you become the writer of a wonderful play, the play of your life: now, near now, future possible. The very structure itself builds in relational vibes because everyone has all had these three levels of blue dots. They might not recognize them, but they have them. Your audience will relate because they've faced obstacles, they've worked with others, and they want to do meaningful work in their life.

When you relate in this way, you get positive outcomes. When you tell your PeakStory and someone responds, it's going to create lots of energy. It's like two musicians who have tuned themselves to show up in the world the way they ought to. You've gone through a deep experience of reflection that strings together your identity in a way that allows it to play it to and from with others. But you're the lead musician. It's *your* tune that energizes the interaction.

If others know you, they have a reason to trust you. That's human nature. And if they trust you and your story has worth embedded in it, you have positive value points. They're on fire to support you, to refer you, to hire you, to be around you because nobody wants to be around people who aren't really uplifting.

Remember what we said about energy? You either take it from me or you give it to me.

Well, I'm a giver. I hope I've given you energy to fire up your own exploration process. Remember what I always say, me search is the best research. Well, now you know this statement rings true. You have proof!

Use this book over and over again. Go back to it. Tear the

pages, bend the pages, dog-ear the thing—even though Mom always told you not to do it—and go for it. This book can become your PeakStorytelling artifact. It's part of your path, your life. If you keep a supplemental journal, great. But feel free to make notes on this book. Track your progress. Make it look like it was an explorer's map back in the day.

We've explored the PeakStorytelling method, the mental flight backward, the check-in with the now, the imagined way forward. If you want to change yourself, change your story; then your brain changes and your story perpetuates that change. It's a way to achieve what Abraham Maslow called psychic hygiene. You feel like you've scrubbed some of the stuff out that was blocking the way, and you have a clear path.

You'll continue to collect blue dots. The virtuous moments will keep arriving. You'll continue to spiral up toward a peak.

In the physical world, humans are naturally attracted to mountain peaks (I'm writing this conclusion at the base of Mount Greylock, the highest point in Massachusetts). I spent some time with a man at the National Braille Press annual gala in Boston who had become consumed with scaling mountains. Erik Weihenmayer, the blind adventurer, has climbed all the world's major peaks, including Everest. Erik is an outstanding speaker when he recalls his climbing achievements or trips like his journey down the Colorado rapids, but some of the stories stand out.

It's the same for everyone. The blue dots we use in our Peak-Story can survive the moment. They stick with people long after the storytelling or speech has wrapped up, long after the circus has left town.

Think about how a story can live on in this way. It has the effect of creating a positive halo and a kind of "stickiness" that helps it remain active inside the listener's brain. It changes their neurology a bit, which is how stories can impact not just individuals but also whole rooms, careers, our home lives, and our relationships with others. Our brains seem to enjoy effective storytelling.

Whenever you rethink your story, commit to it, and tell it, consider this statement from another Erik, Erik Erikson, the American German psychologist known for his theory of human development: "I am what survives me."

If your story is powerful, it will linger after your telling. Whether it's about your immigration from Cambodia, standing up to a bully or of being one yourself, or your…well, you name it (which, by the way, you already did when you identified your blue dots).

Whatever your story, it will linger in the room. It will be planted in the audience's minds, hydroseeded to grow an accurate image of you that compellingly demonstrates your value and worth. It follows your path in an animated manner linked to the work you are doing, your job, the school you are applying to, or the change you are about to make or are already successfully navigating.

As Erikson says, we are what survives us. And your story does just that. It survives you.

# REFERENCES

Anderson, C., and A. Shirako. "Are Individuals' Reputations Related to Their History of Behavior?" *Journal of Personality and Social Psychology,* 94, no. 1 (2008): 320–333.

Aron, A., E. N. Aron and D. Smollan. "Inclusion of Other In the Self-Scale and the Structure of Interpersonal Closeness." *Journal of Personality and Social Psychology,* 63, no. 4 (1992): 596–612. http://dx.doi.org/10.1037/0022-3514.63.4.596.

Ashforth, B. E. *Role Transitions In Organizational Life: Anti-Identity-Based Perspective.* Mahwah, NJ: Lawrence Erlbaum, 2001.

Ashforth, B. E., and F. Mael. "Social Identity Theory and the Organization." *Academy of Management Review,* 14 (1989): 20–39, doi:10.5465/AMR.1989.4278999.

Bailey, F. G. "Gifts and Poison," In F. G. Bailey (Ed.), *Gifts and Poison: The Politics of Peputation.* Oxford, United Kingdom: Blackwell, 1971. 1–25.

Bakhtin, M. M. *Speech Genres and Other Late Essays* (V. W. McGee, Trans.) Austin: University of Texas Press, 1996.

Banathy, B., and P. Jenlink. *Dialogue As a Means of Collective Communication.* New York, NY: Kluwer Academic/Plenum, 2005.

Bass, B. M. "Two Decades of Research and Development In Transformational Leadership." *European Journal of Work and Organizational Psychology*, 8, no. 1 (1999): 9–32.

Bateson, M. C. *Willing to Learn: Passages of Personal Discovery*. Hanover, NH: Steerforth Press, 2004.

Becker, H., and J. Carper. "The Elements of Identification with an Occupation." *American Sociological Review*, 21 (1956): 341–348.

Bennis, W. *On Becoming a Leader* (Rev. ed.). New York, NY: Basic Books, 2003.

Billett, S. "Relational Independence Between Social and Individual Agency In Work and Working Life." *Mind, Culture and Activity*, 13, no. 1 (2006): 53–69, doi:10.1207/s15327884mca1301_5.

Blau, P. M. *Exchange and Power In Social Life*. London, United Kingdom: Wiley, 1964.

Block, P. *Community: The Structure of Belonging*. San Francisco, CA: Berett-Koehler, 2009.

Boje, D. M. *Narrative Methods for Organizational Communication Research*. London, United Kingdom: Sage, 2002.

Boje, D. M. "Using Narrative and Telling Stories." In D. Holman and R. Thorpes (Eds.), *Management and Language: The Manager As a Practical Author* . Thousand Oaks, CA: Sage, 2002. 41–53.

Boycee, M. E. "Organizational Story and Storytelling: A Critical Review." *Journal of Organizational Change Management*, 9, no. 5 (1996): 5–26.

Brett, J. M. "Job Transitions and Personal and Role Development." *Research in Personnel and Human Resources Management*, 2, no. 1 (1984): 155–183.

Brewer, M. B., and W. Gardner. "Who Is This 'We'? Levels of Collective Identity and Self-Representations." *Journal of Personal and Social Psychology*, 71, no. 1 (1996): 83– 93.

Bromley, D. B. *Reputation, Image and Impression Management*. New York, NY: Wiley, 1993.

Bruner, J. *Acts of Meaning*. Cambridge, MA: Harvard University Press, 1990.

Bugenthal, J. F. T. "Objectives Outlined." *Phoenix: Newsletter of the American Association for Humanistic Psychology*, 1, no. 1 (1964): 1.

Burger, P. L., and T. Luckman. *The Social Construction of Reality: A Treatise In the Sociology of Knowledge.* New York, NY: Random House, 1966.

Burke, P. J. "Identities and Social Structure: The 2003 Cooley-Mead Award Address." *Social Psychology Quarterly*, 67, no. 1 (2004): 5–15.

Burnier, D. "Other Voices/Other Rooms: Towards a Care Centered Public Administration." *Administrative Theory and Praxis*, 25, no. 4 (2003): 529–544.

Burt, R. S. *Brokerage and Closure: An Introduction to Social Capital*. New York, NY: Oxford University Press, 2005.

Butler, J. K. "Toward Understanding and Measuring Conditions of Trust: Evolution of Conditions of Trust Inventory." *Journal of Management,* 17 (1991): 643–663, doi:10.1177/014920639101700307.

Cairns, F. "An Approach to Husserlian Phenomenology." In F. Kersten and F. Zaner, (Eds.), *Phenomenology: Continuation and Criticism*. The Hague: Martinus Nijhoff, 1973. 223–238.

Campbell, J. *The Hero with One Thousand Faces*. New York, NY: Pantheon Books, 1949.

Campbell, S. M., et al. "Relational Ties That Bind: Leader-Follower Relationship Dimensions and Charismatic Attribution." *Leadership Quarterly*, 19, no. 5 (2008): 556–568.

Carroll, B., L. Levy, and D. Richmond. "Leadership As Practice: Challenging the Competency Paradigm." *Leadership*, 4, no. 4 (2008): 363–379, doi:10.1177/1742715008095186.

Cavallo, K., et al. "A Practitioner's Research Agenda: Exploring Real World Applications and Issues." In V. U. Druskat, F. Sala, and G. Mount (Eds.), *Linking Emotional Intelligence and Performance at Work: Current Research with Individuals and Groups.* Newark, NJ: Lawrence Erlbaum, 2006. 245–266.

Chalofsky, N. "An Emerging Construct for Meaningful Work." *Human Resource Development International,* 6 (2003): 69–83.

Clark, E. "It's Time for Storytelling: A Proven Management Communication Tool" (2005). Retrieved from http://www.corpstory.com/blog/articles/story-telling-a-proven- technique/.

Cohen, L., and M. Mallon. "My Brilliant Career? Using Stories as a Methodological Research Tool In Careers Research." *International Studies of Management and Organization,* 31, no. 3, (2001): 48–68.

Cohen, P. "Autobiography and the Hidden Curriculum Vitae." (2006). Retrieved from http://www.uel.ac.uk/cnr/cohen.doc.

Colbry, S. "Dynamic Resolve Model: An Interpersonal Resilience Construct." *International Journal of Entrepreneurship and Small Business,* Inderscience Enterprises Ltd, 36, no. 4 (2019): 408–429.

Conforti, M. *Threshold Experiences: The Archetype of Beginnings.* Brattleboro, VT: Assisi Institute Press, 2008.

Conley, C. *Peak: Why Great Companies Get Their Mojo from Maslow.* San Francisco, CA: Jossey-Bass, 2007.

Cooley, C. H. *Human Nature and the Social Order.* New York, NY: Scribner, 1902.

Cortazzi, M. *Narrative Analysis.* London, United Kingdom: Falmer, 1993.

Cottingham, J. (Ed.). *Descartes: Meditations on First Philosophy.* Cambridge, United Kingdom: Cambridge University Press, 1996.

Coutu, D. L. "How Resilience Works." *Harvard Business Review,* 80, no. 5 (2002): 46–51.

Cunliffe, A. L. "Managers as practical authors: Reconstructing our understanding of management practice." *Journal of Management Studies*, 38, no. 3 (2001): 351–371.

Cunliffe, A., and M. Eriksen. "Relational Leadership." *Human Relations*, 64, no. 1 (2011): 1425–1449.

Daft, R. *The Leadership Experience* (3rd ed.). Mason, OH: Thomson, 2005.

D'Aveni, R. *Hypercompetition: Managing the Dynamics of Strategic Maneuvering*. New York, NY: The Free Press, 1994.

Davis, M. "Touchscreen" (2011). Retrieved from: https://genius.com/ Marshall-davis-jones-touchscreen-annotated.

Deci, E., and R. Ryan. "The Support of Autonomy and the Control of Behavior" [Special issue]. *Journal of Personality and Social Psychology*, 53, no. 6 (1987): 1024–1037.

Denning, S. *A leader's guide to storytelling* (Rev. ed.). San Francisco, CA: Jossey-Bass, 2011.

Dowling, G. R. "Reputation risk: It is the board's ultimate responsibility." *Journal of Business Strategy*, 27(2) (2006): 59–68.

Duhigg, C. The power of habit: Why we do what we do in life and in business (Reprint ed.). New York, NY: Random House, 2014.

Dutton, J. E., L. M. Roberts, and J. Bednar. "Pathways for Positive Identity Construction at Work: Four Types of Positive Identity and the Building of Social Resources." *Academy of Management Review*, 35, no. 2 (2010): 265–293.

Dweck, C. *Mindset: The New Psychology of Success*. New York, NY: Ballantine Books, 2006.

Eagleman, M. *Livewired: The Inside Story of Our Changing Brains*. New York, NY: Pantheon Books, 2020.

Ehrich, L. "Revisiting Phenomenology: Its Potential for Management Research." In *Proceedings: Challenges or Organisations in Global Markets*. Oxford, United Kingdom: British Academy of Management Conference, 2005. 1–12.

Emerson, R. M. "Power-Dependence Relations." *American Sociological Review*, 27 (1962): 31–41.

Erikson, E. H., and J.M. Erikson. *The Life Cycle Completed*. New York, NY: W. W. Norton, 1996.

Eteläpelto, A., et al. "Students' Accounts of Their Participation in an Intensive Long-Term Learning Community." *International Journal of Educational Research*, 43, no. 3 (2005): 183–207, http://dx.doi.org/10.1016/j.ijer.2006.06.011.

Fairhurst, G. T. *The Power of Framing: Creating the Language of Leadership*. San Francisco, CA: Jossey-Bass, 2010.

Fairhurst, G. T., and R. Sarr. *The Art of Framing, Managing the Language of Leadership*. San Francisco, CA: Jossey-Bass, 1996.

Ferrin, D. L., et al. "Can I Trust You to Trust Me? A Theory Of Trust, Monitoring, Cooperation, and Intergroup Relationships." *Group and Organizational Management*, 32 (2007): 465–499.

Flum, H. "Dialogue and Challenges: The Interface Between Work and Relationships in Transition." *Counseling Psychologist*, 29, no. 1 (2001): 259–270.

Ford, J. D. "Organizational Change as Shifting Conversations." *Journal of Organizational Change Management*, 12, no. 1 (1999): 480–500.

Fredrickson, B. "The Role of Positive Emotions in Positive Psychology: The Broaden-and-Build Theory of Positive Emotions." *American Psychologist*, 56, no. 1 (2003): 218–226.

Fukuyama, F. *Trust: The Social Virtues and the Creation of Prosperity*. New York, NY: Simon & Schuster, 2005.

Gallup Engagement Survey. "Employee Engagement on the Rise in the US" (2018). Retrieved from: https://news.gallup.com/poll/241649/employee-engagement-rise.aspx.

Gardner, H. *Changing Minds: The Art & Science of Changing Our Own Minds and Others.* Boston, MA: Harvard Business Press, 2004.

Gardner, H. *Five Minds for the Future.* Boston, MA: Harvard Business Press, 2007.

Gargiulo, T. L. *Making Stories: A Practical Guide for Organizational Leaders and Human Resource Specialists.* Westport, CT: Quorum, 2002.

Gargiulo, T. L. *The Strategic Use of Stories in Organizational Communication and Learning.* Armonk, NY: M. E. Sharpe, 2005.

Gecas, V. "The Self Concept." *Annual Review of Psychology,* 8 (1982): 1–33.

Gergen, K. J. *Realities and Relationships: Soundings in Social Construction.* Cambridge, MA: Harvard University Press, 1994.

Gergen, K. J. The Saturated Self: Dilemmas of Identity in Contemporary Life. New York, NY: Basic Books, 1994.

Gergen, K. J. *An Invitation to Social Construction.* London, United Kingdom: Sage, 1999.

Gergen, K. J. *Relational Being: Beyond Self and Community.* Oxford, United Kingdom: Oxford University Press, 2009.

Gibbons, D. E. "Friendship and Advice Networks in the Context of Changing Professional Values." *Administrative Science Quarterly,* 49, no. 1 (2004): 238–262.

Gibson, P. "Where to from Here? A Narrative Approach to Career Counseling." *Career Development International,* 9, no. 2 (2004): 176–189.

Giddens, A. *Modernity & Self-Identity: Self and Society in the Late Modern Age*. Stanford, CA: Stanford University Press, 1991.

Giorgi, A. *The Descriptive Phenomenological Method in Psychology: A Modified Husserlian Approach*. Pittsburgh, PA: Duquesne University Press, 2009.

Gladwell, M. *Blink! The Power of Thinking without Thinking*. New York, NY: Little, Brown, 2005.

Gold, J. "Telling Stories to Find the Future." *Career Development International*, 1, no. 4 (1996): 33–37.

Graen, G. "Post Simon, March, Weick, and Graen: New Leadership Sharing as a Key to Understanding Organizations." In G. Graen and A. J. Graen (Eds.), *Sharing Network Leadership*, vol. 4. Greenwich, CT: Information Age, 2006. 269–279.

Graen, G. B., and M. Uhl-Bien. "Relationship-Based Approach to Leadership: Development of Leader-Member Exchange (LMX) Theory of Leadership Over 25 Years: Applying a Multilevel Multidomain Perspective." *Leadership Quarterly*, 6 (1995): 219–247.

Grutter, J. "Developmental Career Counseling." In J. M. Kummerow (Ed.), *New Directions in Career Planning and the Workplace* (2nd ed). Palo Alto, CA: Davies-Black, 2000. 273–306.

Gubrium, J. F., and J.A. Holstein (Eds.). *Handbook of Constructionist Research*. New York, NY: Guilford Press, 2008.

Habermas, T., and S. Bluck. "Getting a Life: The Emergence of the Life Story in Adolescence." *Journal of Personality*, 72 (2000): 508–539.

Hall, D. T. *Career In and Out of Organizations*. Thousand Oaks, CA: Sage, 2002.

Harley, K., and E. Reese. "Origins of Biographical Memory." *Developmental Psychology*, 35 (1999): 1338–1348.

Hatch, M. J., and M. Schulz. "Building from Theory to Practice." *Strategic Organization*, 3, no. 3 (2004): 337–348.

Heil, G., W. Bennis, and D. Stephens. *Douglas Mcgregor, Revisited: Managing the Human Side of Enterprise*. New York, NY: Wiley, 2000.

Hein, S. F., and W. J. Austin. "Empirical and Hermeneutic Approaches to Phenomenological Research in Psychology: A Comparison." *Psychological Methods*, 6, no. 1 (2001): 3–17, doi:10.1037/1082-989X.6.1.3.

Hermans, H. J., H. Kempen, and R. J. P. Van Loon. "The Dialogical Self: Beyond Individualism and Rationalism." *American Psychologist*, 47, no. 1 (1992): 23–33.

Hollander, E. "Leadership and Social Exchange Processes," in K. J. Gergen, M. S. Greenber and R. H. Willis (Eds.), *Social Exchange: Advances in Theory and Research*. New York, NY: Plenum, 1980. 595–629.

Hooker, K., and D. P. McAdams. "Personality Reconsidered: A New Agenda for Aging Research." *Journals of Gerontology: Psychological Sciences*, 58, no. 1 (2003): 296–304.

Horan, R. "The Integral Psychological Profile: A Psychometric Anomaly Based on Ancient Chinese Wisdom." (2001). Retrieved from: https://www.academia.edu/32375275/The_Integral_Psychological_Profile_a_Psychometric_Anomaly_based_on_Ancient_Chinese_Wisdom.

Hosking, D. M. "Not Leaders, Not Followers. A Post-Modern Discourse of Leadership Processes." In B. Shamir et al (eds.), *Follower-Centered Perspectives on Leadership: A Tribute to the Memory of Meindl*. Greenwich, CT: Information Age, 2007. 243–263.

Hosking, D. M., and I. E. Morely. *A Social Psychology of Organizing*. Chichester, United Kingdom: Harvester Wheatsheaf, 1991.

Hoyt, T., and M. Pasupathi. "Blogging about Trauma: Linguistic Markers of Apparent Recovery." *Electronic Journal of Applied Psychology*, 4, no. 2 (2008): 56–62, http://dx.doi.org/10.7790/ejap.v4i2.106.

Hseih, T. *Delivering Happiness: A Path to Profits, Passion, and Purpose*. New York, NY: Hatchette Books, 2010.

Husserl, E. "Consciousness As Intentional Experience." In D. Moran and E. Husserl (Eds., F. Kersten, Trans.), *Ideas Pertaining to a Pure Phenomenology and to a Phenomenological Philosophy*. The Hague, The Netherlands: Martinus Nijhoff, 1983. 51–81. (Reprinted from *General Introduction to a Pure Phenomenology*, Dordrecht, Netherlands: Kluwer, 1913, 33–34.)

Ibarra, H. "Provisional Selves: Experimenting with Image and Identity in Professional Adaptation." *Administrative Science Quarterly*, 44, no. 1 (1999): 764–791.

Ibarra, H. *Working Identity: Unconventional Strategies for Reinventing Your Career.* Cambridge, MA: Harvard University Press, 2003.

Ibarra, H., and R. Barbulescu. "Identity as Narrative: Prevalence, Effectiveness, and Consequences of Narrative Identity Work in Macro Work Role Transitions." *Academy of Management Review*, 35, no. 1 (2010): 134–154.

Ibarra, H., and K. Lineback. "What's Your Story?" *Harvard Business Review*, 83, no. 1 (2005): 64–71.

Ibarra, H., and J. Petriglieri. "Identity Work and Play." *Journal of Organizational Change Management*, 23, no. 1 (2010) 10–25.

Ibarra, H. "Provisional Selves: Experimenting with Image and Identity in Professional Adaptation." *Administrative Science Quarterly*, 44, no. 1 (1999): 764–791.

Ibarra, H. *Working Identity: Unconventional Strategies for Reinventing Your Career.* Cambridge, MA: Harvard University Press, 2003.

Janson, A. "Extracting Leadership Knowledge from Formation Experiences." *Leadership,* 4, no. 1 (2008): 73–94.

Jefferson, G. "A Case of Precision Timing in Ordinary Conversation." *Semiotica*, 9, no. 1 (1973): 47–96.

Johnson, M. G., and T. B. Henley. *Reflections on the Principles Of Psychology: William James after a Century.* Hillsdale, NJ: Erlbaum, 1990.

Jones, R., J. Latham, and M. Betta. "Narrative Constructions of the Social Entrepreneurial Identity." *International Journal of Entrepreneurship*, 14 (2008): 330–345.

Kaye, B., and B. Jacobson. "True Tales and Tall Tales: The Power of Organizational Storytelling." *Training & Development*, 53, no. 3 (1999): 45–50.

Kegan, R. *The Evolving Self: Problem and Process in Human Development*. Cambridge, MA: Harvard University Press, 1982.

Kim, D. H. *Introduction to Systems Thinking*. Waltham, MA: Pegasus, 1999.

Kreiner, G. E., E. C. Hollensbe, and M. L. Sheep. "Where Is the Me Among We? Identity Work and the Search for Ultimate Balance." *Academy of Management Journal*, 49, no. 1 (2006):1031–1057.

Kroger, J. "Identity Development During Adolescence." In G. R. Adams and M. D. Beronksy (Eds.), *Blackwell Handbook of Adolescence*. Malden, MA: Blackwell, 2003. 205–226.

Kyratezis, A. "Language & Culture: Socialization through Personal Storytelling Practices." *Human Development*, 48 (2005): 146–158.

Leary, M. R. *Self-Presentation: Impression Management and Interpersonal Behaviors*. Madison, WI: Brown and Benchmark, 1996.

Levinas, E. *Basic Philosophical Writings*. Bloomington: Indiana University Press, 1996.

Levi, R. "An Inquiry into a Phenomenon of Collective Resonance." Unpublished paper. 2001.

Linde, C. *Life Stories: The Creation of Coherence*. New York, NY: Oxford University Press, 1993.

Louis, M. R. "Surprise and Sense Making: What Newcomers Experience in Entering Unfamiliar Organizational Settings." *Administrative Science Quarterly*, 25, no. 1 (1980): 226–252.

Maslow, A. *Self-Actualization and Beyond*. Brookline, MA: Center for the Study of Liberal Education for Adults, 1965. Retrieved from Eric database. (ED 012056).

Maslow, A. *Maslow on Management*. New York, NY: John Wiley & Sons, 1998.

May, R. *Man's Search for Himself*. London, United Kingdom: W. W. Norton, 1953.

May, R. *Love and Will*. New York, NY: W. W. Norton, 1969.

May, R. *Courage to Create*. New York: NY: W.W. Norton, 1975.

McLean, K. C., and A. Thorne. "Identity Light: Entertainment Stories as a Vehicle for Self-Development." In D. McAdams, R. Josselson and A. Lieblich (Eds.), *Identity and Story: Creating Self in Narrative*. Washington, DC: American Psychological Association, 2006, 111–128, http://dx.doi.org./10.1037/11414-005.

Mead, G. H. *Mind, Self and Society*, Chicago, IL: University of Chicago Press, 1934.

Merleau-Ponty, M. *Phenomenology of Perception* (C. Smith, Trans.). New York, NY: Routledge (1995). (Original work published 1962.)

Miller, P. J. "Personal Storytelling in Everyday Life: Social and Cultural Perspectives," In R. S. Wyer (Ed.), *Knowledge and Memory: The Real Story*. Hillsdale, NJ: Lawrence Erlbaum, 1995. 177-184.

Miller, R. L. *Researching Life Stories & Family Histories*. Thousand Oaks, CA: Sage, 2000.

Mitroff, I., and R. Kilman. "Stories Managers Tell: A New Tool for Organizational Problem Solving," *Management Review*, 64, no. 7 (1975): 18–28.

Parker, M. "Dividing organizations and multiplying identities." In K. Hetherington and R. Munro (Eds.), *Ideas of Difference: Social Spaces and the Labour of Division*. Malden, MA: Blackwell, Oxford, 1997. 114–138.

Pasupathi, M. "The Social Construction of the Personal Past and its Implications for Adult Development." *Psychological Bulletin*, 127, no. 1 (2007): 651–672.

Pasupathi, M., E. Mansour, and J. Brubaker. "Developing a Life Story: Constructing Relations Between Self and Experience in Autobiographical Narratives." *Human Development*, 50, (2007): 85–110, doi:10.1159/000100939.

Pearson, C. *Awakening the Heroes Within: Twelve Archetypes to Help Us Find Ourselves and Transform Our World.* San Francisco, CA: Harper, 1991.

Pentland, B. T. "Building Process Theory with Narrative: From Description to Explanation." *Academy of Management Review*, 24, no. 1 (1999): 711–724.

Polkinghorne, D. E. "Narrative and the Self-Concept." *Journal of Narrative and Life History*, 1, no. 1 (1991): 135–153.

Rebelo, D. "Phenomenological Storytelling: How Identity-Based Leadership Stories Serve as an Approach to Integrate Self and Work-Place Narratives." Doctoral Dissertation, 2015. Retrieved from Dissertations and Theses database. (3711821).

Seligman, M. *Authentic Happiness: Using the New Psychology to Realize Your Potential for Long Lasting Fulfillment.* New York, NY: ATRIA, 2002.

Seligman, M. *Flourish: A Visionary New Understanding of Happiness and Well Being.* New York, NY: Free Press, 2012.

Simmons, A. *The Story Factor: Inspiration, Influence, and Persuasion through Storytelling.* Cambridge, MA: Basic Books, 2006.

Sluss, D. M., and B. E. Ashforth. "Relational Identity and Identification: Defining Ourselves through Our Work Relationships." *Academy of Management Review*, 32, no. 1 (2007): 9–32.

Staik, A. "The Neuroscience of Changing Toxic Patterns." Blog post. 2011. Retrieved from: http://integral-options.blogspot.com/2011/11/athena-staik-phd-neuroscience- of.html.

Stryker, S. *Symbolic Interactionism*. Caldwell, NJ: Blackburn Press, 1980.

Stryker, S., and R.T. Serpe. "Commitment, identity Salience, and Role Behavior: A Theory and Research Example." In W. Ickes and E. S. Knowles (Eds.), *Personality, Roles and Social Behavior.* New York, NY: Random House, 1982. 199–218.

Towers Perrin. "Understanding What Drives Employee Engagement," 2003. *The 2003 Towers and Perrin Talent Report.* Retrieved from: http://www.keepem.com/doc_files/Towers_Perrin_Talent_2003(TheFinal).pdf.

Towers Watson. "Tracking People Priorities and Trends in High-Performance Companies: Five-Year Employee Opinion Trends in High-Performance Organizations," (February 2014). Retrieved from: http://www.towerswatson.com/en-US/Insights/IC- Types/Ad-hoc-Point-of-View/Perspectives/2014/tracking-people-priorities-and- trends-in-high-performance-companies.

Turkle, S. *Alone Together*. New York, NY: Basic Books, 2011.

Turkle, S. *Reclaiming Conversation: The Power of Talk in s Digital Age*. New York, NY: Penguin Books, 2015.

Van Maanen, J. *Identity Work: Notes on the Personal Identity of Police Officers*. Paper presented at the Annual Meeting of the Academy of Management, San Diego, 1998.

Van Maanen, J., and E. Schein. "Toward a Theory of Organizational Socialization." *Research in Organizational Behavior*, 1 (1979): 209–264.

Wocher, D. *Making the Invisible Visible: Organization Development Practitioners' Interactive Drama in Forming a Sense of Professional Identity*. Doctoral dissertation. 2012. Retrieved from Dissertations and Theses database. (3432491).

Wong, S. S., and W. F. Boh. "Leveraging The Ties Of Others To Build A Reputation For Trustworthiness Among Peers." *Academy of Management Journal*, 53, no. 1 (2010): 129–148.

Wrzesniewski, A., J. E. Dutton, and G. Debebe. "Interpersonal Sensemaking and the Meaning of Work." *Research in Organizational Behavior*, 25, no. 1 (2003): 93–135, doi:10.1016/S0191-3085(03)25003-6.

Zahavi, D. *Subjectivity and Self-Hood: Investigating The First Person Perspective.* Cambridge, MA: The MIT Press, 2005.

# ACKNOWLEDGMENTS

## FAMILY

I am thankful for the companionship of my wife, Shannon, who was an objective sounding board through each phase of the writing process. To my children—Alex and Abby—for their willingness use the PeakStorytelling model as they make their way through their own lives. To my parents for watching me discern life and allowing me to do it my way—even as a kid—and to Jay and Sandy Ryan for their positivity and curiosity in how this work was moving through production into book form. To my grandmother, Maria Alice, for continuing to share her stories with me.

## SCHOOLS

To my University of Rochester faculty, staff, classmates, and Lambda Eta friends, where I first learned how to think about the world more deeply. Thank you to Raymond Murphy and Barbara Ilardi, who invited me into rich conversation, research, and community, and Ed Deci who introduced me—through his teaching—to the essences of self-determination theory. To Saint Raphael Academy for providing a safe and nurturing environment for me to begin to understanding the concept of identity.

To Duquesne University for bringing phenomenology into my life.

To Saybrook University and Thomas Greening for encouraging me through his on-the-spot storytelling recollecting his time with Abe Maslow and Rollo May. I have to thank Amedeo Giorgi, who engaged me to become skilled in using the descriptive phenomenological method in conducting my research. It's been an honor to have his insights and feedback during this journey. To Dennis Jaffe, JoAnn McAllister, Nancy Southern, and Chip Conley, whom I met during my Saybrook University experience and with whom I have fueled relationships ever since.

To researchers, academics, practitioners, and friends from the International Human Science Research Conference (IHSRC). In particular, I'd like to thank Scott Churchill, Rebecca Lloyd, and Celeste Snowbar for welcoming me to the IHSRC at the University of Ottawa.

To my colleagues, past and present, at Roger Williams University. Thank you to Gena Bianco and Jamie Scurry for seeing all of the areas for my work to be woven into the fabric of University College. To Ame Lambert for inviting me to be part of DEI initiatives, which led me to another trusted colleague and advocate, Wanda Heading-Grant, who leads diversity initiatives at the University of Vermont. To Roger Williams University's President Ioannis Miaolas and Provost Margaret Everett, thank you for your continued support and interest in my work.

## COLLEAGUES AND CLIENTS

To James Lawrence for his endless friendship, counsel, and advocacy.

To those who trust me and who have shared their work-life integration efforts with me, our work together has energized me through this process: Joe De Sena, Barnaby Bullard, Kristen Schreer, James Haught, Joe DiStefano, Tony Collins, Kimberly Kleiman-Lee, Elizabeth Shanley, Serge Bouyssou, Christopher Lisanti, Taino Palermo, André Davis, Margaret McKenzie, MD, Scott Pyle, Joe Wein, Justin Thomas, and Candice Nonas.

To the CVS Diversity Suppliers Executive Learning Series Program participants for sharing their stories and enriching mine.

To Michael Tannenbaum and Paul DePodesta for inviting me into the world of the NFL and MLB, respectively, and to Rob Elwood for his tireless efforts in the Sports Mind Institute project.

To my Vegas crew: Amanda Slavin, Arlene Samen, Tony Hseih, Terra Naomi, David Gould, Rich Roll, and Robin Arzón. I have deep gratitude for the transformational experience we encountered as part of the downtown Las Vegas initiative.

To my NYC culinary crew: Bari Musacchio and Chef Al di Meglio for embodying your stories. And a special remembrance to AJ Pappalardo, who is missed every day.

To my Berkshire crew: Deb and Devon Raber, Josh Mendel, Barbara Malkas, and Kimberly Roberts-Morandi for your innovation and eagerness to integrate StoryPathing™ in support of the students of North Adams, Massachusetts. To the Sprague family, Cynthia Sprague, and the Charisma Fund for their support of our students and educators in the region.

To Darrin Gray, Tyrone Keys, and Chris Draft, thank you for allowing me to share my work with you and your nonprofit endeavors. The power of our divine stories is felt.

To StoryPathing™ Certified Career Coaches, Instructors, and Facilitators: Deeanna Burleson, Adam Latts, Barnaby Bullard, James Monteiro, Nia Monteiro, Joshua Mendel, and Jamie Hamilton.

To the Lioncrest Publishing and Scribe Media Teams: Kacy Wren, Christina Ricci, Rachel Brandemberg, and especially Tim Cooke for his listening ear and discerning heart as I trekked forward to get this book just right.

# ABOUT THE AUTHOR

**DR. DENNIS REBELO** is a professor, speaker, and career coach. He is the creator of the PeakStorytelling model, his research-based method for crafting the narrative of who you are and what drives you and why, utilized by former professional athletes turned nonprofit leaders as well as entrepreneurs, CEOs, guidance professionals, and advisors throughout the world.

Dr. Rebelo, former president of Alex and Ani University and co-founder of the Sports Mind Institute, received the 2020 Thomas J. Carroll Award for Teaching Excellence at Roger Williams University. He currently resides in Rhode Island.